THE
WAR AGAINST POLIO

Other Books by Mary Beth Smith

The Joy of Life, A Biography of Theodore Roosevelt

Healing Manic Depression and Depression: What Works, based on What Helped Me

Praise for *The Joy of Life, A Biography of Theodore Roosevelt*

I just looked at your bio of T.R....and want to congratulate you on some first class work. It seems a perfect, very useful intro to Roosevelt.–Edward J. Renehan, Jr., author of *The Lion's Pride*
–Theodore Roosevelt and his Family in Peace and War

There is no better primer for understanding the man Theodore Roosevelt and what drove him to greatness. A very enjoyable read.

–Thomas Finch

I always wondered why Teddy Roosevelt was carved into Mt. Rushmore. After reading this biography it is no surprise at all. What a tremendous person and how blessed this US of A that we should have such as he was for a leader. His impact on American conservation is incredible even to this day!–Carol A. Gerber

This book chronicles [his] journey in a clear, detailed & "friendly" manner...so compellingly that I found myself reading into the wee hours...several nights in a row!!!

–Coral Sue

THE
WAR AGAINST POLIO

By Mary Beth Smith

Dedicated to Jonas Salk with gratitude

God grant me
the Serenity
to accept the things
    I cannot change,
Courage to change the things
    I can, and the wisdom
    to know the difference.
Living one day at a time;
Enjoying one moment at a time;
    Accepting hardship as the
    pathway to peace.
Taking, as He did, this sinful world
as it is, not as I would have it;
Trusting that He will make all things
right if I surrender to His will;
That I may be reasonably happy
    in this life,
And supremely happy with Him
    forever in the next.

—Reinhold Niebuhr

About *The War Against Polio*

The author's father came down with polio during the epidemic of 1944. This book describes his story of pain, rehabilitation and return to normality as well as inspirational stories of other polio survivors, some more severely paralyzed than he was. Most of these people adjusted well to life after polio. But 30 to 40 years later they started getting what is known as post-polio syndrome which the author's father had also.

Also included is a concise but comprehensive history of polio in 20th century America. In 1916, the crippling disease began in New York City and spread to other parts of the United States. Theodore Roosevelt's county was especially hard hit with a 25% mortality rate. He formed a group of prominent citizens from his town of Oyster Bay and tried to prevent the disease from spreading. Nothing worked. In 1921 his distant cousin Franklin got polio and lost the use of both of his legs. He also was weak in his pelvic area and unable to walk more than a few steps on crutches. He founded a rehabilitation center in Warm Springs, Georgia. By 1926 he realized that he was never going to walk again but felt he could still run for office. In 1928 he ran for Governor of New York and served two terms. In 1933 he became President of the United States. While President he asked his law partner, Basil O'Connor, to head up a charity which provided for patient care and research into the disease. All patients needing money for hospital expenses were cared for. It was the most successful charity ever. It eliminated the need for government involvement.

After World War II, people began to clamor for a vaccine to prevent polio in the new generation of baby boomers. Enter Jonas Salk. By using his intelligence, great leadership skills and hard tedious work he was able to test his vaccine in 1952. In 1954 the vaccine was tested on millions of first, second and third grade children and was found to be safe and effective. In 1962 Salk's vaccine was replaced with Sabin's oral vaccine but that was found to cause polio in a few people. In 2000 the United States went back to the Salk vaccine. The Sabin vaccine is used for the developing world because of inability to afford expensive needles and because immunity can be spread by vaccinated people to the unvaccinated.

Table of Contents

Introduction

Polio is spectacular, the way it strikes, the way it kills, the way it leaves its trademark.

—Robert F. Hall, *Through the Storm*

When I was three years old my grandmother told me I should be nicer to my father because he had had polio. "Haven't you noticed his braces and crutches?" She asked. They hadn't made much of an impression on me. They had been there since my birth. "He works very hard so that he can buy food for you," she continued. "And he works for an organization that is trying to find a cure for his disease." This made me feel guilty for not putting up with his teasing but it also made me think that my father was a very great man.

When I was about eight-years-old I realized that I was the only child I knew whose father had had polio—the only kid whose father was crippled. I started to brag about it.

One Sunday I was called to my parent's bedroom. My father was sitting on the edge of the bed smiling gently. "I hear you are telling everyone that I have polio," he said. "I don't *have* polio. I *had* polio in 1944 when I was 35. You can say that I *had* polio."

My father was a quiet man but when he did speak it was usually to tell funny stories. He could make death sound funny. Most of his stories were true and concerned his mishaps on crutches. These mishaps were very, very funny when told by him.

I thought he was a little strange. He was so quiet he was like a benevolent ghost. Unlike most fathers, he always had a smile on his face. He always ate too much for dinner and then went to his easy chair where he fell asleep in front of the TV.

I didn't appreciate him until he was gone and I was faced with a chronic illness myself. At that time I tried to be more like him: never complaining and trying to function as normally as possible under the circumstances. All of his children tried to imitate his honesty, hard work and integrity.

Growing up with a disabled person leaves you a little sad and with a lot of questions. I wrote this book to find out as much about polio as I could. I wanted to find out if other polio survivors were as funny, smiling, calm and accepting as Dad was. I wanted to know what caused polio; who got it; how painful it was; its' treatments and therapy; the vaccinations. Why did the virus get stronger as it passed from person to person? Why did adults start getting it later in the century? How did victims adapt to their disability? How bad is post-polio syndrome and how close are we to ridding the world of polio?

I learned some things from writing this book:

- Wash your hands frequently.
- Get recommended vaccinations.
- Polio survivors were and are great people.

* To protect their privacy, some people are referred to by their first name and the first initial of their last name.

1. You Have Polio

It had never occurred to me that anything bad might happen to me.

—Charles Mee

Paralytic polio starts with flu-like symptoms, no worse than fatigue and aching limbs. Some polio victims felt well up until the day before the paralysis hit.

Suddenly the person begins to become paralyzed and collapses right where they are standing. My high school history teacher's brother collapsed while getting off the school bus. Dad collapsed while getting out of bed. A brother of a friend of mine was always trying to "fly" down the stair case. When he fell down the stairs because of polio no one paid any attention to the loud noise. They were used to it. He recovered completely but as an older man had post-polio syndrome (PPS) which is explained in chapter 6.

The polio victim was driven to the hospital— one specializing in polio, if possible. Once in the hospital they found themselves "stiff as a board" not able to move a muscle, eat, drink, urinate or defecate. Soon the pain began. Leonard Kriegel, another 1944 victim, heard whimpers, moans and screams the entire time he was in isolation.[1] Dad said it felt like every nerve in his legs were dying—like they were being drilled by a dentist without novocaine. It was the kind of pain that remains forever in your mind. The kind that causes people to hallucinate. Nothing was given for the pain. It was thought pain medication would compromise their breathing. People whose diaphragms had been paralyzed, couldn't breathe and were put in iron lungs. Later, most people would be weaned from the iron lung but some people spent decades in one.

The Acute Stage

My father said he got polio from swimming near boats that were emptying their sewage tanks. But no one really knows for sure. He worked in the crowded conditions of Baltimore city. He could have gotten it from a menu handled by a person who had not washed their hands or from somebody's sneeze or cough.

Even though Dad didn't feel well, he and Mom dropped their two daughters, Anne, age 9, and Sue, age 6, off at their grandparent's summer house on the Chesapeake Bay in Pinehurst, Maryland. Then they drove to Hot Springs, Virginia.

They were supposed to come back on Monday. On Sunday Anne practiced rowing the boat. She wanted to see how far she could row.

Her grandmother called her in and told her the sad news. Dad had the flu and was coming back early. She wouldn't have a chance to row him in the boat.

Meanwhile Mom and Dad had been staying at a luxurious hotel called the Homestead. Rich people went there. There was even a small airport that the hotel guests could fly into. On Saturday they went horseback riding and Dad complained that his legs hurt very badly. On Sunday they ate at an outside buffet but since Dad felt achy and feverish they called Mom's parents and drove back to pick up their two children.

When my parents got back to Pinehurst, Anne pleaded with Dad to let her row him in the boat. At first he said no. He was too sick. With much begging and pleading Anne persuaded him to go out with her in the boat so she could show off her rowing skills. My grandfather took a picture of them rowing—the last time Dad would be able to get into a little boat.

When they got home, he mowed the lawn in spite of his aching legs. Later it was discovered that polio was more likely to paralyze if the person remained active while the virus was incubating. A neurologist said that extreme physical exertion during the beginning of an attack "is almost suicidal, while the continuance of even average physical activity is dangerous." A young man was paralyzed in both arms after paddling a canoe in a race. A parachutist participating in combat training ended up in an iron lung. A violinist lost the use of his left hand while practicing fingering exercises.[2]

Had Dad rested as soon as he felt bad the virus may have passed through his gastrointestinal tract leaving no paralysis. The worst paralysis was in young, active adults. Dad was lucky he did not end up unable to move or breathe like some adults did.

That night Dad was very restless in bed and slept very little. Early the next morning Sue and Anne were giggling over something silly when they heard a loud crash. The giggling stopped. The crash they heard was my father falling to the floor when he tried to get out of bed. He somehow got back in bed and the family doctor was called. The doctor said it was polio.

He was taken to Sydenham, a "contagious disease" hospital where a spinal tap confirmed the diagnosis. He spent the most painful part of his illness there. Then he was transferred to Johns Hopkins for a week or two. He then went to Baltimore's Children's Hospital-School where two well-known physiotherapists worked. He stayed there from October of 1944 to April of 1945.

• • •

One Sunday in 1935, a toddler, Jean W., became very ill. When she became unconscious her father went out to find a doctor. He found two on the golf course. They checked the girl for signs of life and there were none. They pronounced her dead and called an undertaker. While she was *sleeping* she "saw (or dreamed) about a beautiful lady dressed in blue, sitting in a lovely garden." The entire time this was going on a neighbor, who was a nurse, was performing CPR on her. Jean started breathing again before the undertaker could get to the house. Later she wrote that since then, "I've had spiritual guides in the form of two adult men who watch over me."[3]

In 1952 four-year-old Nancy G. felt tired and achy. She was put to bed with a fever. Two days later she tried to get out of bed and fell to the floor.[4]

In 1943 three-year-old Janice K. woke up crying. She couldn't move her arms or legs.[5]

Katalin P., whose family were World War II displaced persons, was in bed with a headache, high fever and neck pain. She walked to the bathroom, her legs and arms tingling. She lowered herself to the floor outside the bathroom, and said, "I can't move...my body is asleep."[6]

In 1949, a 7th grader named Peg Kehret was practicing in a chorus. She felt a twitching muscle in her thigh. Two days earlier she had had a sore throat and a headache. When the bell rang, she started walking towards the lockers and collapsed. She was weak and her back hurt. Nevertheless she walked the 12 blocks home. She went to bed with a severe backache. It was polio.[7]

Thomas R. came down with polio in 1953 at the age of 19 when he and his family went to stay in a cottage that they thought was vacant. There were four boys there mourning the death of their friend from polio. Three of the boys came down with polio. So did Thomas. He became what he called a "breathing-impaired quadriplegic." He spent two years in the hospital. After two or three months he was transferred from an iron lung to a rocking bed.[8]

Jeane Dille

In the 1950s milk bottles were usually delivered to the back porch. When 28-year-old Jeane Dille went to pick up the four bottles, they fell to the floor. Two broke. Her shoulders hurt. She vomited into the toilet. She didn't have the strength to stand. She lay down on the couch and wondered how she was going to be able to take care of nineteen-month-old Linda.

The next day she couldn't go up the stairs and Bill, her husband, fixed up a mattress for her downstairs. They got a babysitter to care for their children. A bed finally opened up at the polio hospital in Battle Creek, Michigan. Polio was diagnosed when a nurse noticed the rigidity of her neck.[9]

She "felt more pain more places than I can describe."[10] Like so many polio victims in the acute stage, she had hallucinations. She saw "clouds of dust" —which themselves didn't exist—turn into visions of famous movie stars and radio personalities. She'd wake up at night and try to chase the communists she was seeing into the bathroom. Every time she did this a nurse had to put her back into bed.[11]

She was fitted with a respirator which covered her from pelvis to shoulders. When her drainage and swallowing problems increased she needed a tracheotomy to create an airway from which phlegm could be suctioned.[12] She was only put into a "twilight state" so her breathing wouldn't be overly compromised. The doctors decided to leave her in her bed while they did the operation. A cloth was placed over her eyes so she wouldn't be able to see what was going on.

Suddenly she felt her body float "near the ceiling." She was able to look down at her body. She saw one doctor watch the operation while Dr. Wencke's "hands moved busily between my neck and the nurse's hands as she offered him requested instruments."

As she watched, she realized that she was being asked to make a decision. What did she want most in the world? She decided she wanted to live long enough to raise her two children. If that was not permitted, she would accept it. Then she found herself back in bed.

Her next memory was of Dr. Wenche rushing into the room. He didn't bother taking precautions—that is, he didn't wash his hands and put on a mask and gown. He just went straight to her bed "bent over, kissed [her] on the forehead, and said 'I didn't think I would see you again,sweetheart.'"[13]

Leonard Kriegel

In 1944 eleven-year-old Leonard Kriegel shared cookies with his new friend Jerry on a bus on its way to camp. They decided to bunk together. One day Jerry complained about a pain in his stomach. Later, he complained about pain all over. He was taken to the infirmary.

Leonard took a nap. When he tried to get up to go to the bathroom, he fell across the bed. He got up and slowly made his way down the stairs to the bathroom where he discovered he couldn't urinate. He went back up the stairs but collapsed on the floor. He was taken to the infirmary where he could hear Jerry "yell and curse, so loudly, so horribly." They were both taken to the hospital where Jerry continued to yell. Jerry died that night.[14]

Leonard wrote later that he was "seventy miles north of New York where I lay board stiff even as the virus charged up from my toes as relentlessly as Babel's Cossack Cavalry."[15]

Charles Mee

Charles Mee thought he got polio on a trip—maybe from a water glass at a restaurant or a door knob at a motel.

On the day his legs began to ache he went on a date. Afterwards he, his date, and some friends met back at the girl's house. Mee found he couldn't make it down the stairs to the club basement. He told the other kids that he was okay and he walked the 15 blocks to his home. He made it home but fell many times on the way. His parents rushed him to the hospital where he felt weak and stiff. He had pain, sweating and hallucinations. He was in isolation for fifteen days.[16]

He wrote:

> *I went from a healthy athletic boy weighing 160 pounds to a frightened child of 90 pounds, unable to move a muscle except for three fingers of my left hand.*
>
> *As the neurons in my body died one by one during those two weeks, I felt relentless pain, like the pain of a tooth being drilled without novocaine, but all over my body. As though a dentist was peeling back my skin, layer by layer, exposing each neuron individually, taking hold of each one with a pair of tweezers, and drilling down the length of it to its root, until he had burned it out. Then starting again, peeling back another layer of flesh, burrowing deeper into my body, going down inside the bone, as I sank deeper and deeper into delirium, surfacing only partly from time to time when some white-clad figure moved through my room.*

He was given nothing for the pain.

"From now on, I can face anything," he told himself later.[17]

Mary Lou D. called her first weeks of polio "four weeks of hell on earth." William F. described it as "constant and intense pain."[18]

Lauro Halstead

Dr. Lauro Halstead got polio while hitch-hiking in Europe. It started with a little diarrhea and he felt like he had the flu. He got on a train. The next day he couldn't raise his right arm above his head to get his luggage. He walked to find a hotel and had to walk up five flights of stairs to get to his room. He collapsed on the bed.

An American doctor came and diagnosed polio and the American embassy called his parents. By pulling strings his mother got on a plane within forty-eight hours.

He was taken to a German nursing home. By the time his mother got there he had started having trouble breathing. He was then taken to a children's hospital where he crammed his 6'4" frame into a child-sized iron lung. That night the electricity went off and he couldn't breathe. He had hallucinations. To save electricity the hospital routinely turned it off for four hours at night. When he was able to breathe for 24 hours outside the iron lung he was allowed to fly back to the United States. The paralysis in his legs and left arm went away but for the rest of his life his right arm would be paralyzed. His switched from being right-handed to being left-handed.
[19]

Lumbar Puncture

To confirm that it was polio a long needle was used to take a sample of spinal fluid. Jim S. who had polio in 1952 said, "[Mom] heard me scream and she suspects it was done without any anesthesia."[20] Ronny D. said, "Years later Mom recalled that she could hear me screaming as she walked all the way down the driveway to the mailbox and back."[21]

• • •

Out of 100 people who got the poliovirus, 95 did not notice it. 5% noticed it but most did not become paralyzed because it never left the gastrointestinal tract. They may have had minor symptoms—fever, headache, sore throat and diarrhea but they thought it was the flu. Some people who got the virus had no symptoms. All of these people were carriers of the disease.

Paralysis can be monoplegia which affects one limb (most common in children); paraplegia which affects both legs (common in both children and adults); tetraplegia which affects all four limbs and is most common in adults. Tetraplegia sometimes spreads from the feet to the legs to the ribcage to the arms and to the diaphragm.[22]

Patients in the acute ward had to be taken care of like babies. They could't urinate or defecate on their own. They couldn't move any part of their body. Iron lungs saved patients who couldn't breathe on their own. Later they might be weaned from the respirator.[23]

Patients would try to move toes, fingers, legs, arms, their bladders, bowels and their sexual organs. When Irving Z. woke up with an erection he "wanted to shout, 'Look at this' to [his] friend in the next bed but was too embarrassed." Peg Kehret scratched an itch and then yelled, "I CAN MOVE MY HAND!!" Soon she could move her hands, arms and legs and feed herself sitting up.[24]

Patient Abuse

15% of all surveyed patients said they were emotionally, physically, or sexually abused. Many female patients were sexually abused.[25] So were some men. One man was repeatedly fondled by a nurse. One young man's pubic hair was shaved by a nurse for an ankle operation. One was frequently examined naked by student nurses.[26]

Hugh Gallagher's bowels were not working and he developed a fecal impaction. Without warning a nurse "reached in and ripped out the fecal matter piece by piece." He felt like he was being raped.

A nurse told nine-year-old Marilyn R. that she would turn her respirator off if she didn't stop crying. When she didn't stop, the nurse turned it off and the child immediately passed out. Someone noticed that it was off and turned it back on.[27]

Vegetables were forced down one child's throat when he wouldn't eat. He was often put out in the sun as punishment and would get a severe sunburn. Sometimes they left him alone in the bath. He was completely paralyzed. Had he slipped down in the bath he would have drowned.[28]

Patients were verbally abused. They were told they would never date, marry or have sex. They were told they were ugly and incompetent.[29]

The food was bad at many hospitals. "The bad food never stops," one patient complained. Hamburgers were "sorry, tasteless, little things." Hot dogs were "hideous" and "green." Nurses pretended not to notice when family members brought in fried chicken, lobster tails and candy. [30]

Modern Sanitation Theory

People in the 19th century were not obsessed with cleanliness. They took a bath once a week and washed their hair with a bar of soap once a month. Once a year they would hang their carpets over the clothes line and beat them with a broom. They washed their clothes once a week which took two days because they had to let them soak for a day. They washed their good clothes less often because they thought washing would wear them out. People still used outhouses. There were open sewers.

Polio existed at that time and some children got it but it is thought that most babies were exposed to it while they still had immunity from their mothers. They were exposed by the time they were six months old and were left with immunity for life.[31]

If occasionally a baby became crippled or died, childhood death was not unexpected. Paralysis was puzzling. Still, it did not cause alarm.[32]

By 1880 many people had indoor plumbing and infants were no longer exposed to the poliovirus. They were unable to make their own antibodies. In 1887 there were 44 cases of polio in Stockholm.[33]

By the 20th century antibiotics wiped out bacteria.[34] Science had minimized or gotten rid of many diseases.

People took good hygiene seriously and few children or babies died.[35]

During World War II American soldiers in the Middle East came down with polio. Polio existed in the Middle East but was not epidemic. Also it was not severe. It only affected one limb and it only struck children. The soldiers didn't have any immunity to polio therefore many of them got it and brought the disease back to the United States.[36]

Dr. Richard L. Bruno disagreed with the modern sanitation theory. He said that the bad epidemic in 1916 started in the filthy slums of New York. Also, in 1908 there was a small outbreak in Massachusetts which started where people had poor sanitation. He also pointed out that from 1938 to 1942 a study showed that polio was 40% more common in the slums of Baltimore than it was in the rest of the city. During the war Europe had terrible hygiene and polio was epidemic there. It was also very bad in Germany where Germans had been hit by bombs and were living in overcrowded conditions.[37]

When Albert Sabin noticed a high rate of polio even in developing countries, he said, "It is quite evident you can have tremendous amounts of paralytic polio...[even where] sanitary hygiene is very bad."[38]

In 1896 Dr. Charles Caverley made a study of the 1894 polio outbreak in Vermont and said, "General sanitary conditions did not seem to have any influence on the epidemic."[39]

Anne Finger, polio survivor, wrote that polio is now prevalent in countries where conditions are filthy. Also as infant and child mortality fell in the late 19th century people began to notice the polio outbreaks more.[40]

Some children got polio after a tonsillectomy which allowed the virus to enter through the exposed nerve endings and go to the Central Nervous System (CNS). Doctors began to postpone such operations until after the polio season was over.[41]

The polio season lasted from approximately early May to Labor Day depending on what part of the country you lived in. During a bad epidemic doctors would pray for an early frost since polio rarely occurred after the first frost. Jonas Salk theorized that the polio season corresponded with the allergy season. Perhaps allergies make it more difficult for the body to fight polio. Jonas Salk was not given time to prove this theory but my father was allergic to many things and he got polio. My mother, who had no allergies, did not.

• • •

1916

In the 1916 epidemic people blamed all sorts of things for polio. They thought cats harbored the infection and 70,000 of them were killed. They thought fleas carried it from person to person. Houseflies which fed on feces were blamed. Bedbugs were blamed. [42] Later it was thought that polio entered through the nose. In 1934 there was an experiment where 4600 children were injected with alum far up into the nostrils. They got a headache and permanently lost their ability to smell.[43]

Italian immigrants were blamed for the 1916 epidemic in New York City. They lived in squalid conditions and kissed the lips of their dead. Movies, camps and pools were closed. Streets were scrubbed wasting 4 million gallons of water a day.[44]

People with children began to flee the crowded cities. People under age 16 had to produce a certificate showing they were free of polio before they could leave the city. Baltimore County and other areas did the same. One family from Pikesville, Maryland had to state that they were healthy and free of polio "and had not been exposed to same."[45]

While a father was driving his polio-stricken boy to the hospital, the boy died. The hospital refused to accept the body. The father drove for hours with the dead body of his son and finally had to leave it at a disinfecting plant.[46]

Oyster Bay Township, Nassau County, NY

In 1916 the township of Oyster Bay, New York had one of the highest incidents of polio in the entire nation. Polio hit mostly young children at that time. The epidemic had started in New York City but the city was linked to Nassau County on Long Island by railroads and steamships. The township of Oyster Bay had large estates where wealthy people summered. It also had hotels and boarding houses for vacationing city dwellers. The biggest draw was the village of Oyster Bay where former president Theodore Roosevelt lived.[47]

Theodore Roosevelt

Theodore Roosevelt was one of the only presidents whose greatness was appreciated while he was still alive. He had a loveable personality. He wrote many books including *The Rough Riders* which describes his part in the Spanish American War. After the war he became wildly popular and became governor of New York. He was pushed into the vice presidency by the corrupt party boss and fate propelled him into the presidency in 1901 when President McKinley was assassinated.

He preserved millions of acres of wilderness for future generations, won the Nobel Peace Prize, built the Panama Canal, arbitrated a coal strike and made laws to protect workers.

In 1912 he ran for president under the Progressive Party and was shot. Only a steel glasses case and a thick copy of his speech kept the bullet from entering his heart.

By 1916 Theodore Roosevelt had retired to Sagamore Hill, his house in Oyster Bay and was spending his time writing articles, letters, and playing with his grandchildren.

Pollution

Oyster Bay was contaminated by raw sewage leaking mostly from the country estates.[48] William J. Burns, the township's health officer was ignored by the town council when he said in May 1916 that the village of Oyster Bay was being threatened by the death of oysters from pollution.

The polio epidemic that had started among Brooklyn's Italian immigrants started to spread to other areas of the United States. Burns proposed cleaning up dirt, dust, and quarantining polio victims. Burns was not trusted because he was suspected of wanting an increase in his piddling salary. [49]

Polio in Oyster Bay Township – July

Parents began to flee New York City to outlying villages and Oyster Bay braced itself for a polio epidemic. On July 7 the first case appeared in Glen Cove in the Oyster Bay township. Four additional children of Italian and Polish descent got polio on July 10th and 12th. On July 10th the Oyster Bay town council forbade all children under the age of sixteen to assemble in public places.[50] At a meeting on July 2nd it was noted that there were 16 cases of polio in the township. A third of them were Italian. There were five deaths.

Inspectors

Inspectors were set up at nearby railroad stations to make sure that every visitor had a certificate of good health. On July 24th Theodore Roosevelt led a group of about 100 prominent men and women from Oyster Bay village to a town meeting and gave a "fiery speech" denouncing health officials for neglecting to clean up Oyster Bay township.

August

On August 1st there were 27 victims. One third of them were from Glen Cove. Children of Italian and Polish descent were taken to an isolation facility know as "Orchard." Only half of them had polio.[51]

The country estates which leaked a huge amount of sewage into Oyster Bay were a big part of the problem but the little guy with his mostly harmless "rubbish heaps" was blamed for spreading the disease.

Theodore Roosevelt was the "thought leader" for a citizen's committee which always immediately acted on his advice. They raised money for a cleanup and the construction of a hospital. The poorer year-round residents, a number of them Italian and Polish, formed a Committee for the suppression of Infantile Paralysis. They dispersed information about polio in English, Italian and Polish. They also distributed garbage cans, hired five nurses to do house-to-house inspections and reimbursed families, who had been quarantined, for lost wages.

In the next two weeks there were forty-one new cases: only two were Italian and eight Polish. By this time people were almost hysterical with fear. Even Theodore Roosevelt, whose grandson Richard was staying with him, was afraid.

State Department of Health

The State Department of Health ordered a survey of Nassau County and made three new regulations. Once a family member had had polio, the house would have to be disinfected. All patients would have to be moved to an isolation hospital and there would be no public funerals for polio victims. A new quarantine facility was built called the Jones Institute in Hicksville in the Oyster Bay township.[52] This may have been due to pressure from Glen Cove residents to abandon the awful "Orchard" facility.

The practice of home quarantine allowed for the more affluent children to recover at home while poor children were carted off to the hospital. Many children with no symptoms were taken to the hospital because they were Italian or Polish.

On August 28, there was an unruly town meeting in Oyster Bay. By that time the total count of polio victims in the township was 100, 73 in August alone. The immigrant population demanded its own sanitary committee. It also demanded that children not be removed from the home without parental consent.[53]

September, October, November

On September 1st the Roosevelt committee dismissed the visiting doctor and the watchmen stationed at five checkpoints. But on September 4th there were three new cases.

The ban preventing children under the age of 16 from assembling was lifted.

On September 15th the Roosevelt committee reported that they had hired workers to remove rubbish and had hired six watchmen to be posted at all entry points to the township. They had engaged a physician and a trained nurse to diagnose polio. They had distributed funds to quarantined households and had collected $5,000 for them and been pledged $5,000 more.

Only a minority of the victims now were Polish or Italian. The U.S. Public Health Service discontinued the inspection of travelers leaving New York City on October 14 but on November 30 six children in Oyster Bay township came down with polio. The final count of polio victims was 130. In Nassau County it was 482 with a 25% mortality rate.[54]

Only 10% of polio victims in the township were Italian and only 18% Polish.. But the upper and middle classes demanded that Italians be taught cleanliness and

Poles stop acting so emotional when their children were being dragged from their homes. Oyster Bay township became known as the "pest hole" of Long Island. What they most needed was a sewage system. Wealthy summer visitors didn't care and the year-round residents didn't think it was fair to pay higher taxes for a sewage system when the raw sewage was produced mostly by the rich.[55]

● ● ●

The Rules

During Charles Mee's childhood there were certain rules they had to follow:

- Don't make new friends. Stick to the old ones whose germs you are used to.
- Stay away from beaches and pools.
- Never use another's tooth brush or drink out of their glass or Coke bottle.[56]

When I was little, my mother gave us enemas (because polio was spread by fecal matter), made us go to bed by eight, and made us take naps during the polio season. A neighborhood pool was finally opened in 1956 after most children had been vaccinated.

Stigma

One writer said, "Everybody was terrified of polio survivors, and even their families for years.[57]

Even after we were vaccinated one of our neighbors hesitated to let us play with her grandchildren because my father had had polio.

Louis Sternburg wrote, "Dottie began to find that neighborhood parents didn't want our children near theirs....I found out years later that, because I'd been at the golf club that Sunday, they emptied the pool and closed the dining room. The Sternburg family were lepers."[58]

Ernie L. said, "After I was diagnosed, our neighbors threw things at Jerry [his brother] and screamed at him to stay away from them and their children."

One survivor said, "My family was shunned and hated by everyone."[59]

Another said, "Now our family, like other 'polio' families, was looked on as 'dirty' by the rest of the world."[60]

Larry K. said, "Some people didn't want their children to play with my brothers because we'd had polio in our house."[61]

One of my friends, Donna S. went with her mother to visit her cousin. Her cousin was sitting on the floor. Donna's mother asked, "Why doesn't she get up?" "She had polio and can't stand," the child's mother said. Suddenly Donna's mother grabbed her hand and they ran out of the house.

However a study in Baltimore found that polio patients were ostracized for a very short time. Once the patient was no longer contagious, the neighbors rallied around the family with offers of help.[62]

What is Polio?

When Linda M. was 10, she slept with her mouth open because she thought polio germs came in through the nose. Everyday she checked herself for the symptoms of polio. Do I have a fever? A headache? Fatigue? A stiff neck or back? Can I breathe okay? Walk okay? The next year they had the Salk vaccine trials and polio soon became a thing of the past.[63]

What was this virus that was feared by so many? It dates back to Egyptian times (1580 BC – 1350 BC.) It's been endemic all this time but not epidemic. The Germans noticed it early and called it kinderlahmung which in English is translated as infantile paralysis. It was called that in the United States until the 1930s when adults started getting it. Then the name was changed to Poliomyelitis which literally means "gray matter in the spinal cord," "myelos" (marrow), and "itis" (inflammation).[64] The disease tears away the myelin sheath that covers some of the motor nerves. When the nerves stopped sending signals to the muscles the muscles would stop working. The older and more active you were, the worse the paralysis.[65]

The disease became more prevalent as the years wore on. In 1894 130 children were paralyzed in Vermont, 18 died. In 1916, in the Northeastern United States, 27,000 were paralyzed and 6,000 died.[66] In 1949 there were 42,000 cases and 2,720 deaths. In 1952 there were 58,000 cases and 3,000 deaths.[67] As it passed from person to person, the disease got more virulent.[68]

There is no cure for polio. Antibiotics are only effective against bacterial infections like pneumonia. It is an almost indestructible virus. The virus no longer exists in the United States because of the polio vaccine. But it is elsewhere in the world and if you are going to travel in that area, it is wise to get vaccinated. The virus is still being studied and we know more about it now.

The poliovirus is a beautifully sculpted sphere with mountains and valleys. There are 60 identical valleys, called canyons or clefts. It is picked up when someone neglects to wash their hands after going to the bathroom and then touches an object which someone else then touches. It is especially dangerous to put your fingers in your mouth. Money, credit cards and restaurant menus all contain fecal matter. Polio is also spread by sneezing and coughing.

For about ten days it grows in the throat and goes into the stomach. At this point, your body may be able to expel it. If not, it makes replicas of itself and is carried to the lymph nodes.[69] A large amount of the virus builds up in the lymph nodes which burst and the virus goes into the bloodstream where it is carried to the brain and spinal cord and latches onto polio virus receptors (PVRs) which the clefts fit into perfectly. It latches onto the large nerve cells called motor neurons in the spinal cord that control the diaphragm, neck, arm and leg muscles. Some of the neurons are no longer able to make neurochemicals and their motor neurons can no longer make the affected muscles contract. Some nerve cells will fight off the virus and survive. They often sprout new connections to the orphaned muscle fibers.[70]

2. Rehabilitation

These are my braces,
They set me free
But, these are my braces,
They are not me.

Without my braces,
I sit in my chair.
Without my braces,
Life is not fair.

But, put on my braces,
And I'm just like the others
Put on my braces,
And I run like my brothers.

Well, not exactly,
I'll have to admit, no.
Well, not exactly,
'cause I had polio.

—Richard L. Daggett, 1954

My father who always wanted the best for himself and his family wanted to go to the best polio hospital in town. That hospital was Baltimore's Children's Hospital-School. The only problem was—that hospital was for children only. He was a thirty-five-year-old man. So he told the National Foundation for Infantile Paralysis (NFIP) that he did not need their money. (He was a proud man.) He only needed their help getting into Children's Hospital. Once he got in, other adults followed.

Henry and Florence Kendall

Henry and Florence Kendall were head of the physical therapy department. They had transformed a run-down hospital for crippled children into a nationally known rehab center for polio. Florence (1910-2006) had helped World War I veterans suffering from nerve and muscle injuries. Then she had gone to Children's Hospital-School and worked there for the next fifty years.[1]

In 1935 she married disabled veteran Henry Kendall (1898-1979). Mr. Kendall had been hit by a shell during World War I which had destroyed one eye and nearly blinded the other. He got his training in physical therapy while attending the Evergreen School for the Blind in Baltimore. I was examined by him in the mid-1960s for scoliosis (curvature of the spine). By feeling he could tell how bad my scoliosis was. He then prescribed exercises for me. Neither I nor other patients could tell he was blind.[2]

After the polio vaccine came out Children's Hospital-School was renamed Baltimore Children's Hospital and its NFIP funded iron lung center was closed.[3] It had been one of the first iron lung centers in the United States.

After Henry died in 1979, Florence became a lecturer and received four honorary doctorates. In 2002 she became a member of the Maryland Women's Hall of Fame. She was named "Physical Therapist of the Century" by the Maryland American Physical Therapy Association Chapter.[4]

War–1941

A friend, Bob M., remembers listening to the radio with his family on the afternoon of December 8, 1941 as President Roosevelt spoke to the nation:

> *Yesterday, December 7, 1941—a date which will live in infamy the United States of America was suddenly and deliberately attacked by naval and air forces of the empire of Japan....Very many American lives have been lost. I ask that Congress declare...a state of war...between the United States and the Japanese empire.*

After the speech was over, each of Bob's four brothers came over to him and said, "I won't be here tomorrow." They signed up to fight the next day. Bob at sixteen was too young to join them.

Older men like my father who had wives and children were not as patriotic. Dad convinced his doctor to give him a deferment which said that he was not qualified for military service due to medical reasons.

Polio–1944

When he first got polio, Dad must have been wondering what he did to deserve this punishment. He must have been mourning the loss of the use of his legs. He would never run again, never fly again and never go boating again. He thought he would never drive again. Dad always tried to find a way to live with the tragedies that happened to him during his life. During the 1960s and 1970s I noticed it only took him two or three days to make peace with (what was to him) the unthinkable. There is no reason to suspect he took much longer than that to get over this misfortune.

Dad believed that if he had fought in World War II, he would have been killed. But he had stayed in Baltimore, practically the polio capital of the world, and had gotten polio. It was ironic. At least he was alive. Somehow he would find a way to walk, even if it was by using crutches.

Having made his peace with polio, he set about helping young men in his ward deal with their illness.

Soon after he was accepted at Children's Hospital-School, other young men were accepted, many were teenagers. There was only one man there older than Dad named Jim Polk. Jim Polk had a wife and his job was being held open for him. The younger men and teenagers were worried. They thought that they would never go to college, never have sex, never get married and never have a family.

Dad would say, "Of course you'll go to college. Polio didn't damage your brain, did it? Of course you'll have children. You're not impotent are you? Someone will marry you. Mrs. Polk and my wife are standing by us and this patient's girlfriend (pointing to a teenager) visits everyday. Plenty of women will find you attractive." One of Dad's young disabled friends, Ecky Boden, did go to college and became a lawyer. Ecky, although severely handicapped, was much more successful than his lawyer father.

I wrote my mother and asked if Dad made friends at the hospital. She wrote back:

> *As far as friends, he was very popular at the hospital. We became friendly with one of the nurses, and visited her and her husband later at their home. Jim Polk, a patient became a good friend along with his wife. Ecky Boden was only eighteen but we have exchanged Christmas cards every year and were very friendly with his parents....Another good friend was Happy Braudenburg who along with her friend was a therapist in the pool. We also exchange Christmas cards and she has invited me to visit her in North Carolina. Except for Jim Polk, most of these friends were younger people.*

Jeanne Dille, twenty-eight-years-old when she got polio said, "We had the kind of camaraderie that I imagine exists between soldiers who have fought together during a long and difficult war. In our case, the enemy was polio." According to quadriplegic Louis Sternburg "the best thing about life in the rehab center was the

companionship that developed among the patients."
They grew "very close."[5] They developed a sense of
community. They talked about their hopes and fears
and tried to come to terms with their illness. They joked
about the quality of the food and the lack of sex. Admir-
ing a nurse they'd say, "I'm ready, willing, and *unable.*"
[6] These patients as well as the physical therapists were
by far better psychologists than the psychiatrists were.
One physical therapist told a patient to stop saying "I
can't." "Always express yourself in the positive." She
also warned the woman that men don't often stay married to handicapped women. However women were
likely to stay married to handicapped men. (She was
correct.) One psychiatrist asked a mother who was in an
iron lung how it felt to know she'd never hug her children again. The woman broke into tears and cried all
day. Another asked Lou Sternburg who was in an iron
lung also, "How's your sex life, Lou?" "Terrific," he answered. "How's yours? What kind of dumb question is
that? Are you trying to shock me? Cut the crap, Doc."[7]

Others wrote about their problems accepting polio. Author Charles Mee had wanted to be a college football
player, maybe a professional.[8] Psychiatrist and writer
Arnold Beisser at age twenty-four had won a national
tennis championship. At the young age of twenty-three
he had completed medical school. Yet in 1950 he was
flat on his back in an iron lung, thinking, "Strong and
able, I could not possibly be a cripple! I would not have
it."[9] He thought he'd be able to play table tennis after
getting out of the iron lung but since his arms and legs
were paralyzed, that was an impossible dream. Like
other victims he "searched [his] memory to recall what
crime [he] had committed that would merit this punishment." He kept trying to find "that fatal flaw."[10]

Twelve-year-old Peg Kehret had always wanted to be a writer. Now she couldn't hold a pen or use a typewriter. She was also worried she'd never get married. "Who would want to marry a woman who couldn't go to the bathroom alone?" she wondered.[11]

Twenty-eight-year-old Jeane Dille had had big shoulders, big muscles and a deep chest. Before polio she had been able to swim five miles. With her weakened muscles she'd never be able to swim again.[12]

Children also blamed themselves for the illness thinking they had run too much, played too hard, or wore out their legs riding their bikes.[13] One child thought she had gotten it because she pulled her dog's ears. One mowed the lawn when it was too hot. One ate blue berries he was not supposed to eat. One fell down when he was playing too rough. One went out to play when he was told not to.[14] One girl said she grew up feeling "different" and "less than." She was ashamed of her skinny legs, her limp, her "weak stomach muscles and after the surgery, my inflexible back."[15]

Patients hoped for the best but doctors were forced to give them the awful news. When one told Hugh Gallagher that he would never walk again without assistance, he shut down all feelings for years. Other patients never got over their depression.[16]

In July of 1955 Louis Sternburg, a young married man with two children, asked "When am I going to walk out of here?" The doctor said, "We, er…We don't believe you'll ever walk again, Lou. And I may as well tell you that I don't think you'll ever breathe again without mechanical assistance." "You son of a bitch, you're lying!" Lou screamed. "One of these days I'm going to walk into your office and smack you right in the teeth!"[17] He said later that, at the worst, he had expected to be confined to a wheelchair.[18]

Some polio victims, many lying helpless in iron lungs, had mystical experiences which vary for different people but can involve a feeling of timelessness along with a feeling of being lifted up. For the seconds it lasts, all pain is gone. It can bring a sudden turn around in the person's thinking. They may be able to free themselves of their neurotic tendencies (which we all have) or addictions. No one knows what causes this experience. William James, who wrote *The Varieties of Religious Experiences,* said:

> If the fruits for life of the state of [mystical experience] are good, we ought to idealize and venerate it, even though it be a piece of natural psychology; if not, we ought to make short work with it, no matter what supernatural being may have infused it.[19]

Dad's Physical Therapy

Dad told my mother that first Henry Kendall measured his muscle ability and prepared a treatment plan. Other therapists massaged his legs every day. Also there was water therapy which included massages and movement of his limbs under water. Water therapy stimulated blood circulation and made the body lighter.[20]

On January 16, 1951 a program called *The Fight Against Polio* appeared on television. It was part of a series produced by Johns Hopkins called *Science Review Series.* It demonstrated the latest therapies for polio at Baltimore's Children's Hospital-School.

Muscle Testing

Henry Kendall was shown testing a woman's right shoulder while his wife, Florence, narrated. It was below 50% normal ability or, as Mrs. Kendall said, *in the red*. The right arm was tested and had good strength. Mr. Kendall tested finger strength to see whether she would be able to type or play the piano. Then the woman's thumb was tested. "There is no loss of function," Mrs. Kendall said. Mr. Kendall next checked the wrist. The muscles in the wrist were good. The patient could bend it back and forth. All of Dad's muscles were tested at first but after that particular attention was paid to his legs. One leg was stronger than the other but eventually he had to wear braces on both.

Pool

Dad would have been placed on a bed, lifted up by pulleys and lowered into a small pool of warm water where the therapist, Happy Braudenburg, was waiting. He would have laid in the water while Happy raised his leg and rotated his hip. She would have also moved his knees, feet, ankle muscles and toes.

Once he got a braces and was more confident balancing himself he would have been able to walk in the water without braces, tip-toe at first but later walking normally

Wheelchairs and Braces

Dad would have been given a wheelchair at first. People loved the mobility wheelchairs gave them. "I was free now," Leonard Kriegal said, "freer, as far as the adult world was concerned, than I had ever been before."[21]

Dad was delighted when he got his new braces. They would, with practice, make him "independently mobile." He would be able to do things he would not have been able to do from a wheelchair. He would be able to go up and down stairs, even if they didn't have a railing, sit down and get up from all kinds of chairs and sofas, get into and out of automobiles, sit down and get up from a toilet seat.[22]

Dad practiced walking with crutches and braces over and over until he became quite skilled at it. For the rest of his life he appeared proud of his careful, skillful—if slow—method of walking. He never complained about the heaviness of the braces or how tired crutch walking made him feel.

Leonard Kriegel who got polio at age eleven pestered his brace maker, "When do I get mine Charlie." "Soon, Lennie," he grunted. "Soon." "They heavy?" "You got arms, no?...So they ain't heavy. You'll learn. Sooner or later, you all learn."[23]

Peg Kehret got walking sticks which were shorter than crutches and had a ring of metal which went on a patient's arm just below the elbow. [24]

Anne Finger complained that while she had access to most buildings, the crutches often caused "pain and fatigue....often wearing out one's fragile joints."[25]

Dad had a pair of wooden crutches which he didn't use much. They put too much pressure on his underarms and would have eventually caused numbness in his hands. He usually used aluminum crutches which had a cuff around his arms to hold the crutch in place. More recently, people buy designer crutches "sleek, lightweight fire engine red." [26]

Respirators

I scream
The Body electric,
This yellow, metal, pulsing cylinder
whooshing all day, all night
In its repetitive dumb mechanical rhythm.

—Mark O'Brien, *The Man in the Iron Lung*

Children's Hospital-School had one of the first iron lungs. It also had a rocking bed. Air was pumped into iron lungs. When the patient's body had to be attended to, port holes in the iron lung had to be opened so that nurses could reach in. Since patients could not breathe well with the port holes open, a new feature was added. A dome was slapped in place to cover the patient's head and make it easier to breathe. Then the iron lung was pulled out so that the entire body could be exposed and attended to.

There were also respirators for babies which held two infants. These respirators could also be turned into incubators..

Some people wore respirators around their chest made of plexiglass.

By 1951 iron lungs and rocking beds were arranged around a television set at Children's Hospital-School which the patients much appreciated.

The modern iron lung was built in 1928 by Philip Drinker for people whose diaphragms had been paralyzed. Others had built crude iron lungs before so he isn't considered its inventor. Its push-pull motion forced the diaphragm to expand and contract. It was a steel cylinder three feet in diameter and seven feet long. It weighed a third of a ton. In 1929 60 to 80% of patients died in it. Then it was discovered that secretions had to be sucked out of the patient's pharynx to prevent pneumonia.[27] In 1932 John Haven Emerson invented a lighter, cheaper iron lung whose entire top was hinged. This one was produced in the thousands.

Some people died in it after a few weeks. Others only needed occasional help breathing. Some were able to leave the iron lung permanently. Some lived in the iron lung until they died of old age—the record was Julie Middleton of Melbourne, Australia who lived in one for sixty-one years and died at the age of eighty-three.[28]

In 1938 Aubrey Burstall invested the cuirass which was a respirator that could be worn outside the clothes allowing patients to go outside and travel by bus or train. Today they are made of light weight fiberglass and have compact pumps.

The rocking bed was invented by Jesse Wright. The bed tilts like a seesaw and allows the head to go up and down at a 45 degree angle. The guts are pushed into the diaphragm so that air can be moved in and out of the lungs.

In the 1950s a modern "intermittent positive pressure ventilator" pushed air directly into the trachea. It reduced mortality to 20% and is in routine use today.[29]

Coming Home

Dad came home for a short time Christmas of 1944 and stayed for about two weeks. He laid on a hospital bed in the living room and received friends and relatives. Anne and Sue played with him and sat on his bed and talked to him.

After nine weeks in the hospital Jeane Dille came home for a visit and found herself in pain and sensitive to the touch. She became exhausted and glad to get back to the hospital.[30]

Once the doctor wrote "no further recovery in musculature is to be expected," the patient was free to go home, with frequent visits back to the hospital for therapy.[31]

Hospital stays averaged eight months.[32] My father stayed nine months. But some little children stayed for many years.

Sister Elizabeth Kenny

In the early 1960s I peeked into the den where my father was watching an old movie on television. He looked over at me and said, "Sister Kenny." I said, "What?" and he repeated "Sister Kenny." He was a man of few words. Why waste his breath telling me who she was when I could simply sit next to him and watch the movie? This was why he never explained what *gesundheit* meant. It was simply what Dad said every time one of us sneezed. What more did we need to know? He explained SPAM by giving us a taste of it— braunschweiger, ritz crackers, cheese-whiz, matzos, sardines and pickled herring the same way. What other explanation did we need? The fact that some of these had funny names only added to our (and his) delight.

Rosalind Russell played the part of Sister Kenny, the Australian bush nurse who began to develop a method of treating polio patients while treating her first one in

1909. When Miss Russell came across the patient she wired a doctor, described the symptoms and asked what the disease was. The doctor wired back, "Infantile Paralysis. No known treatment. Do the best you can with the symptoms presenting themselves." Miss Russell used gentle massage and heat to help the pain. Later she used exercise. In no time at all, the child recovered and walked during a very stirring scene. And that is all I remember about the movie.

In reality, Kenny visited the child every day to offer sympathy and therapy. After the acute stage of the disease was over, the child, like many, regained his strength and was able to walk again.

Among other things, Kenny preached the abandonment of immobilization with splints and casts. Splints and casts caused the patient's healthy limbs to atrophy.

A report from a royal commission studied her method and said "that any system of treating poliomyelitis that disregards the use of immobilization will reap a harvest of spinal deformities such as have not been seen since the days when the disease was treated on less logical lines."[33]

Kenny was invited to teach and demonstrate her work at Queen Mary's Hospital, Carshalton, England.

She went back to Australia during a severe epidemic in the State of Victoria. A report was published stating that "deformities from muscle imbalance had not materialized but had in their splinted patients." Kenny's patients, it was also noted, did not appear as "stiff." "The reason why," they said, "should be earnestly sought."

After the report was submitted, Kenny treated acute cases at the Brisbane General Hospital. Finally, in 1939, it was publicly admitted that her treatment worked in the acute stage.[34]

In 1940 the father of a former patient advised her to come to the United States. Sister Kenny a large, mannish-looking sixty-year-old woman wearing an old-fashioned wide brim hat topped with flowers, didn't look a thing like the beautiful Rosalind Russell. She annoyed doctors by saying that all atrophy and paralysis came from not following her instructions. The first time she met Basil O'Connor he listened to her but refused to promote her ideas. Tom Rivers, a virologist from the Rockefeller Institute for virus research, said he couldn't stand her. O'Connor said later, "I think she's a crackpot, but I'm not so sure she may not have something."

She carried on her work at the City Hospital, Minnesota and at the University of Minnesota Hospital, Minneapolis. She also went to other centers, gave lectures and demonstrated her therapy. She visited and taught her treatments in New York and in Winnipeg.[35] She was very popular in the United States. Her accent was considered lower-class in Australia where doctors described her as "uncouth." But Americans, who love any accent that sounds vaguely British, thought it was intriguing.

People thought she could restore paralyzed muscles to fully functioning muscles. Instead, what she was doing was exercising good, healthy, atrophied muscles to normal use. The muscles had remained still for a long time either because the patient was afraid it would hurt to move them or because they had been in splints. She called the atrophy "alienated muscles" and used other terms confusing to doctors.[36] She also said polio was a disease of the muscles when every doctor in the United States knew polio was a disease of the nerves.

Her Therapy

First Kenny would do a cleansing enema, then a hot pack treatment for the pain. Then a gentle massage was done which also relieved the pain. Then she stretched the muscles which was painful but kept healthy muscles from atrophying. Splints, used for years to prevent deformities, were discarded.[37] Farmers began to use them as beanpoles.[38]

At first she'd move the patient's muscles herself. Then, as the patient got better, he would actively move what muscles he could (and even try to move muscles he couldn't) while visualizing the muscle being exercised.[39]

Kenny rejected the rush to surgery. Orthopedic surgeons used surgery in an attempt to normalize the child's appearance. They tried to make the child's "bad" leg appear as if it was growing along with the child's "good" leg. This was done until the 1960s and was considered butchery decades later. It was very painful and involved months spent in and out of hospitals.

Reports of her work were good and physical therapists and nurses went to the University to study her methods. As a result of her work the NFIP funded the University of Minnesota.

In January of 1941 the National Foundation for Infantile Paralysis (NFIP) sent five nationally recognized physical therapists to study her method. Two of them were Henry and Florence Kendall of Baltimore. They listened to her lecture and watched before and after slides of patients. Florence noted that Kenny used unscientific words to describe polio. "There was a confusion of terms," Florence said. She felt that all of Kenny's cases would have recovered anyway and that the muscle spasm Kenny was referring to "recovers very quickly."

Kenny invited the five therapists to lunch. Henry and Florence had a prior commitment and couldn't go. After lunch, Kenny gave a demonstration of her work. The three therapists who watched it were impressed with her compassion and also noticed that the patients became calm as they visualized the movements of their muscles.[40]

Everyone but the Kendalls, who had missed the demonstration, were impressed. Patients in the acute stage of polio actually did get better faster using Kenny's therapy.[41] Physical therapists were impressed. Doctors, too, quickly came to the conclusion that immobilization caused healthy limbs to become disabled.[42]

By 1943, the NFIP started funding courses in the Kenny method[43] and people began to consider the Kendall method too conservative.[44] However the Kendalls remained anti-Kenny.

A nurse who caught polio while working at the Baltimore Children's Hospital-School felt she wasn't improving very fast. By telling her story to a newspaper she was able to get moved to Minneapolis. Her father wrote that her improvement under Kenny had been "unbelievable." Her mother said that Kenny was an "inspiration" to her.[45]

John Pohl, the shy superintendent of the Kenny Institute, said her work was "the finest and best treatment known at the present time," and wrote a book to clearly explain it.[46]

There was almost universal acceptance of her methods in the United States. Most doctors used her suggestions—heat, hydrotherapy, muscle reeducation, massage, avoiding immobilization and postponement of orthopedic surgery. For pain, some hospitals used warm, but not hot, packs. Some doctors agreed with her that if muscle testing was done too early it caused unnecessary pain. Many agreed that surgery on children was done far too often and her muscle stretching didn't hurt anybody.

In 1949 she claimed to be sixty but was really pushing seventy. She moved to Toowoomba in southeastern Queensland and wrote her second autobiography *My Battle and Victory* which was published after her death.[47] She had a stroke and was treated with a new blood thinner. It didn't work. She died November 30, 1952.[48]

3. Coming Home

Society expected polio survivors to never complain or express self-pity. They were expected to find a career that would challenge anyone.

—Kathryn Black

Dad came home in April with crutches and a hip to ankle brace on his left leg. Walking very slowly he walked to the back porch and went into the kitchen. There was a wheelchair waiting inside for him. He gradually gained strength until he could walk pretty well, visiting Children's Hospital-School periodically for checkups and therapy.

Dad was worried about finding a job he could do. He had enough money to live on for some time but originally intended to use it for his retirement. He knew he needed to be around people. He had left a number of friends in the hospital and would have no one to talk to and entertain if he stayed home. My mother didn't appreciate his sense of humor which was his greatest asset. He thought he could never go back to his old job which entailed much driving. How could a person who was crippled drive a standard shift car?

Then one day he went for a checkup and saw a friend quickly swing through his crutches and get into his car. Then he drove away! The next time he saw his friend he asked him how he did this. He offered to fix Dad's car so that he could drive. He fastened rods to the clutch and the brake so that they could be worked by hand. Dad was able to use the accelerator since his right foot and leg were okay. He was able to go back to work.

He was lucky. Many disabled older people had to look for work that they were capable of doing.

Jeane Dille

Jeane Dille took her wheelchair home with her. She was too weak to care for her children. She had to make daily visits to physical therapy and was delighted to discover she could drive there by reaching through the steering wheel with her strong left hand to shift. (Her right shoulder and arm were weak.)[1]

When invited to a party she found sitting up uncomfortable and asked if she could lay down. They were rarely invited back to that person's home perhaps because of her husband's obvious embarrassment.[2]

To shop all she had to do was order from the free Sears catalog.[3] She was also able to work. After he husband divorced her she got a top clerical position at a local telephone company. A neighbor helped with her children while she was at work. She later got a job at an insurance company. She remarried in 1965 and went back to school while working part time. She got a PhD and taught for many years.

Children

Children did well if they were expected to help out around the house. They washed dishes and did other chores that didn't require much walking. Some children were "able to do most anything other children did as long as it didn't involve running or climbing trees."[4]

Schools were difficult for children. There were no elevators and the flights of stairs were steep. Children tried to excel in class work to make up for their disability.

Jim D. went to a school for disabled kids. He discovered many new interests—politics, music, theatre and study. He went onto college and obtained a professional career.[5]

Bullying and Child Abuse

Before Glen H. was born and while his mother was pregnant his father threw his mother over the back of the sofa. She landed on her belly. He was a breech baby. The doctors had to hit him so hard to get him to breathe that they broke his legs. After he got polio in 1949 his father would hit his mother if she tried to comfort him. He would say, "Leave him alone. It will make him a man."[6]

Many parents hit polio victims. Charles W. had a violent step-father but most of the time his mother intervened. Mothers also hit children who they felt had been spoiled by the nurses.[7] One boy's father beat him up and said he wished polio had killed him. One father beat his daughter if she tried to use a wheelchair instead of her crutches. A mother screamed at her child, "Why are you doing this to me?" One boy's father and sister kicked and slapped him because he couldn't help out on the farm.[8]

Anne Finger's father could go into a rage when he was drinking. Once he dragged her into the living room onto the sofa and began to choke her. She thought he would stop but he didn't. He kept choking her and banging her head against the arm of the sofa. She usually allowed him to do what he wanted until he petered out. But this time was different. This time she knew he was going to kill her. She tried to fight. Finally she managed to say, "Mommy! Mommy! Help! Help!" That made him stop. Her mother appeared in the doorway and said, "Don't upset your father."[9]

Marcia H. got polio in 1951 but recovered almost completely. But a classmate of her's wore leg braces. She said, "Life was hard for him. Kids can be cruel—and teasing him or avoiding him was easier than being kind."[10]

A boy who wore a brace on his right leg was "beat up a lot." Kids would ask, "How dare you try to be like us?"[11] One boy on crutches "was constantly challenged to fight, and often kids broke his glasses when they would knock him down and throw his crutches out of his reach. Then the kids would run away."[12]

Children who had gone into the hospital as toddlers came out emotionally fragile, dependent and irritable. If their stay had been long their speech development was slowed.[13]

Anne Finger

Anne Finger, who was on crutches, had the attitude of so many polio survivors. She had "made a compact.... with the world—not to complain, to be a good sport, to soldier on, not to whine, to just keep going."[14]

While taking night classes at Harvard, she had to give herself one extra hour to find a nearby parking space "close enough that I could manage the walk, and then half an hour to walk my slow, slow walk from the car to my class."[15]

Like others, Finger was afraid of slipping on ice. "I was used to going through the winter with a good collection of bruises from slipping on ice....Climbing stairs had never been any more difficult for me than walking—it was just another activity that I accomplished a lot more slowly and with a lot more effort than everyone else around me."[16]

Anne Finger would often become fatigued from crutch walking. She would walk from the bus stop "two and a half blocks up the hill, passing Catalpa Road and Ivy Street and then letting myself in the back door of our house, so exhausted that I would throw my crutches and coat onto the living room floor and collapse on the couch."[17]

• • •

Teenagers found it difficult to get dates. Terrified of rejection, they stayed home. Many teenagers went to college because they couldn't get jobs that required physical work. John L. said, "Any work I would do in the future would have to be of the sedentary type."[18]

One teenager felt ostracized in groups of kids his own age. His parents found him crying about it one day and helped him avoid those situations.

One patient became a successful lawyer and later worked on making buildings accessible for people with disabilities.[19]

Most of the polio survivors became employed. One quadriplegic became the chief executive officer of a corporation. Another became director of the New York City Mayor's Office on the Disabled. Most survivors married, had children and had four years of college as opposed to the high school education the average American had.[20]

Louis Sternburg

If a person had breathing problems the family had to convert a room in their house to a hospital room with an iron lung and/or rocking bed.[21]

Louis Sternburg was completely paralyzed and couldn't breathe on his own. If he wanted to go out he had to do frog breathing which is using the tongue to push air down the throat to the lungs.[22] He was in constant pain.

His relatives were generous, but he didn't want to rely on them for money so he started up his old business of selling woven labels that go on clothes and say such things as *dry clean only*. He found a way to use the telephone to make sales calls and his wife kept the records, did the book keeping and wrote letters. Making phone calls helped him forget his pain.[23]

After years passed he found it was too much of an effort to go out. The last straw was his wife's birthday party. She gave him a cracker and he choked on it. She had to work on him for thirty minutes to get him breathing better. Finally he said, "Take me home." He became depressed and, except for two times, didn't go out for another fifteen years.

In spite of his depression, he was able to concentrate and pay endless attention to detail. But, said his wife,

"He was quite unlike his old self, very negative about everything and very demanding and tyrannical."

A psychologist helped him to deal with his feelings of helplessness, dependency, anger and fear of abandonment. He learned to develop trust in his nurses and attendants and allow his wife to go out.[24]

His wife said of him in the mid 1980s, "He still meets a lot of people and is always making new friends....They love to be with Louis because he makes them feel good, and he has the gift of knowing how to draw them out to talk about themselves, and then to listen."[25]

Arnold Beisser

Arnold Beisser was an M.D. but since both of his arms and both of his legs were paralyzed and he tired easily he would have to find a specialty that was physically easy on him. He began to imagine himself as a psychiatrist and began to read about the subject.

As he began to meet more people in the hospital, he realized people liked him and accepted him. He began to visualize himself as a sexual being. He knew the first step would have to be dating a woman.[26]

Arnold met a nurse in the hospital and they got married. Since he could breathe best sitting up he got married alternating between lying flat and sitting up. As a psychiatrist, he managed by sitting up for as much as two hours after which he became exhausted.[27]

Arnold did well as a psychiatrist. Eventually he had to give it up and started writing amazingly insightful books.

Leonard Kriegel

Leonard Kriegel, who became a writer, came home after two years fat and soft.[28] "The first thing that I remember doing after I arrived home was to get out of my chair and walk through that small apartment in the Bronx on my braces and crutches."[29] Friends, neighbors and relatives met at his house, talking to his mother as if he was not there. "Is he going to go to school," someone asked. "Maybe you should move to an elevator apartment," someone else said.[30]

He started to spend a lot of time daydreaming about being a baseball hero. He spent a lot of time feeling guilty about being so much trouble to his mother. Children, bums, veterans and old ladies saw him as a fellow sufferer and confided in him.

One day, he realized he was a cripple and started crying. Then he felt "a growing knot of hate," and resolved to change his fat into muscle. His hate changed to "dry, hard rage." He wanted to get even. It was, he said, "a time when I set about proving to the virus that I could function as well on braces and crutches as others could on legs."[31]

He walked miles on braces and crutches, did hundreds of push-ups everyday, dips on the monkey bars for hours and worked out at home. He visualized his heroes: Hemingway, Peter Reiser, F.D.R., Henry Fonda and Gary Cooper.

He now excelled at crutch-walking:

> *My body began to make its own moves. It adjusted. It came to know its enemies—the curbstone that was just a half-inch or so too high to take*

> *on the swing-through gait, the dry leaf or piece*
> *of paper lying carelessly in the street, waiting for*
> *my crutch, the thin sheet of ice that wasn't vis-*
> *ible unless I walked slowly, eyes searching the*
> *pavement beneath me for the secret of balance,*
> *the drops of water on a marble hallway or tile*
> *bathroom....*
>
> *At least I could manage by myself now. I could*
> *climb up and down stairs; I could go for a walk*
> *of a few blocks or so; and when we went away*
> *to the country for two weeks in the summer, my*
> *mind, if not my body, was admired.* [32]

His psychic pain began to slip away. He wrote later, "A crutch walker knows that he *needs* those braces strapped to his legs and those crutches beneath his shoulders—but they are *his* legs on which he is standing. And he *is* standing."[33]

He said, "It was ultimately the need to prove myself an American man, tough, resilient, independent, and able to take it, that pulled me through my war with the virus."[34]

At 17, he wondered how a cripple could make love to a woman. He went to a movie to try to find out. It was called *The Men* starring Marlon Brando who played a paraplegic. He admired how well Marlon Brando handled the wheelchair. But what he really wanted to know was, "How did a cripple have intercourse?" But no movie made in 1949 was graphic enough to answer his question.[35]

• • •

After Lawrence B. had polio, he began to date but felt that many of them were *mercy dates*. In 1965 he married.

"Because my leg was paralyzed, I wondered if it would affect me otherwise—like being able to perform sexually. My wife was understanding, patient and accepting. Obviously it worked." They had two daughters.[36]

Charles Mee

Charles Mee resented the many offers of help he received. He disliked the pity implied. "Pity is what we feel for those who are hopelessly inferior to ourselves," he said. He didn't want to be defined by "what I couldn't do rather than what I could." He said:

> *When I was first at home, I negotiated the stairs up to my bedroom, by turning around, sitting down, and going up on my butt. And when my mother asked if she could help by taking my crutches for me, I would say, "No, thanks, I can do it myself." And when she asked if she could help me reach a book or turn on the television or get out of the car or put on a shoe, I would say patiently, 'No, thanks,' or sometimes I would snap at her that I could do it myself. Hundreds of things were decided in this way, hundreds of ways in which I would be dependent or not, hundreds of ways in which I would adapt.[37]*

• • •

A housewife who was a polio survivor could cook, clean and stand with leg braces to wash dishes. She socialized and had two more children. "Mom never let anything slow her down," said her daughter Nancy.[38]

Mary Bready of Baltimore already had a family and polio only affected one leg. She looked at it as a challenge and learned to walk without a brace.[39]

Bill Warwick could only move "the fingers on one hand slightly and wag a foot." He spoke to groups challenging them to use their mobility while they still had it.[40]

Hank Steputis got polio in 1953. He could breathe eight hours a day and used a rocking bed to rest and sleep. He was able to do telephone sales from home.[41]

One quadriplegic unable to breathe on his own timed television commercials for a living.

Thomas R. was confined to a rocking bed. He depended on his parents. "I realized I took a lot of their life," he said later. "My father had a good enough job that he could support me." Still, Thomas felt like he was slowly going crazy. So he started a securities business which really took off after 1964. Over the years he was able to hire helpers so that he would not have to solely rely on his parents. He had a bus driver, a live-in student and an aide he could confide in.[42] In 1987 he started having difficulty breathing. It felt like something heavy was sitting on his chest. He died at age 60.[43]

Lauro Halstead got polio when he was a college student traveling in Europe. Polio left him with a frail right arm. He learned to use his left hand. In 1957, three years after he had gotten polio, he climbed Mount Fugi. He became a doctor and saw patients, did research and raised a family. He now works at the National Rehabilitation Hospital in Washington, D.C.[44]

Painters who lost the use of their dominant hand had to learn to paint with their other hand. Henriette Wyeth

Hurd had to hold the brush between her first and second fingers. Some people learned to paint with their feet. Heather Strudwich, a mouth painter could only leave her iron lung for a few hours a day.[45]

A New York Yankees pitcher, Bud Daley's right arm became shorter and weaker than the left. He learned how to throw left-handed. Other people who had polio include Olympic runner Wilma Rudolph, golfer Jack Nicklaus, bicyclist Conrad Duke and Olympic gold medalist in figure skating Tenley Albright.[46]

Dr. Linda Jane Laubenstein had polio in the early 1950s, severe asthma and was confined to a wheelchair. Her practice consisted of mostly AIDS patients. She helped organize the Kaposi's Sarcoma Research Fund and the first full-scale medical conference on AIDS. She died in 1993 of a heart attack.[47]

Violinist Itzhak Perlman and cellist Pierre Fournier had polio. So did singers Connie Boswell, Walter Jackson, Neil Young and Joni Mitchell.[48] Ray Peterson, who wrote the song "Tell Laura I Love Her," had polio.

Elizabeth Twistington got polio in 1953 and was almost completely paralyzed. She spent her nights and most days in an iron lung. She wrote books and did mouth paintings and drawings. She founded the Chelmsford Dancers.

Many survivors took up photography. Lord Snowden (Tony Armstrong Jones) who had polio in 1946 at age 16 was a famous photographer.

Francis Ford Coppola who became ill at age 11 created puppet shows and made an 8-millimeter movie while recovering.[49]

Stephen Dwoskin who had polio at age 10 studied the human body and made motion pictures of paralyzed bodies.[50]

Mark O'Brien earned a college degree and wrote and published essays, poems and his autobiography.[51]

Peg Kehret, who had polio as a child, wrote many books most of them for children. "Perhaps I like to write from the viewpoint of a twelve or thirteen-year-old because I remember that time in my life so clearly," she explained.[52]

Many survivors wrote books, some about their experiences with polio:

The Unbeaten Track	Arthur Tarnowski
Of Men and Mountains	William O. Douglas
Long Road Back	Edward Le Comte
Game-Legs	Arthur Bartletts
My Last Days as Roy Rogers	Pat Cunningham Devota
In My Heart I'm Still Dancing	Elaine Strauss
The Lung	J. G. Farrell
It Can't Happen to Me	Enid Foster Green
Door to the Sea	Erick Berry
Rise Up and Walk	Turnley Walker
Abandoned Child	Mary Morgart
Passage through Crisis	Fred Davis
Out of the Ordinary	Robert Lovering
Missing Pieces	Irving Kenneth Zola
Looking Up	Jane Boyle Needham
The Raging Moon	Peter Marshall

• • •

There were the "hidden costs" of polio. Dad set up a work bench in the basement for building model airplanes and ships. With the help of John Stewart, his young cousin, he put in a bathroom with an old claw-footed bathtub. On the first floor he turned a closet into a small bathroom with a shower. (He had to have a bathroom on every floor and became nervous if you stayed in *his* bathroom too long.) John also came every Saturday to help Dad do any other work he needed him to do. He helped remodel the basement when it flooded ruining the paneled walls. A friend showed Dad how to modify his car so that he could drive. Someone built a ramp to the porch door while Dad was still using a wheelchair. When he fell trying to walk on his braces and broke his leg, a retired doctor from next door was called and some neighbors put him back in his wheelchair. After that happened a second time he became much more careful.

One survivor's father designed and built a one story ranch house with "wider doors and other adaptions."[54]

Other people modified their current home and changed or bought a new car. My father bought the first car available with automatic transmission in 1948, an Oldsmobile.

Effect of Polio on the Family

Dad tried to do everything for himself. Of course we had to do little things like hold the door for him and change the channel on the TV. We didn't mind doing these things because we knew he had been dealt a hard blow. We were happy to do the little he asked.

In the 1940s Anne remembers him visiting his friends who had had polio. She said he was well-known in polio circles and was frequently being called upon to speak about the March of Dimes.

When Franklin Roosevelt died, she was playing outside with two friends. She was shocked and hurt when they said they were glad he was dead. They were the children of rich Republicans who resented what F.D.R. had done for ordinary people.

She says he would bowl from a wheelchair, played badminton and at least once went to the beach with tennis shoes on his crutches. He always tried to ignore the polio. He set up his Pontiac with hand controls so that he could use the clutch and bought the first car with automatic transmission—an Oldsmobile. He always bought Pontiacs and Oldsmobiles up until the end of his life.

Drinking was dangerous for him. It made him fall down at at least three parties and he learned to drink less so that this wouldn't happen. At home, he and Mom drank crème de menthe. He loved to eat candy and this drink was sweet like that.

Before the three younger children were born, she remembers hearing our parents having sex. While the noise disturbed her, she was glad Daddy could *do it*. She figures that was when I was conceived.

After I was born she was asked to design her own bedroom in the attic. The baby had taken over her room. She looked in a magazine and found a picture of built in drawers, shelves and closets and told Dad that was what she wanted. She helped him finish off the attic. She put in shutters, walls and storm windows and put insulation in the walls which she now thinks was asbestos. While they were putting in the insulation, Dad wore a scarf around his nose and mouth because of his asthma and bronchitis but didn't give one to her.

• • •

Lou Sternburg was a quadriplegic who couldn't breathe on his own. His son accepted his father's condition as a given because he had been only two-years-old when his father got polio. He liked that his father was always in the same room when he came home from school. He liked sitting and talking to him. He had to drop whatever he was doing if his father needed his body shifted or his nose scratched. He felt bad that his father was "always in pain. Always."

Lou's daughter took it for granted that Daddy might ruin the family's plans to go out. Her mother would say, "If he doesn't feel good, we might not be able to go."

They began to have parties and cookouts at home. "I realized," she said, "we were working together as a team to overcome what had happened to Daddy."

Their mother had been shy and hesitant before Lou got polio but she changed afterwards. "What she says, goes," her daughter said.

Kathryn Black's father had been needy and dependent on his wife. Her mother had always been attracted to the underdog. Her father couldn't handle her complete helplessness and left before she died in her rocking bed. Black's grandparents raised Kathryn and her brother.[55]

Humor

Arnold Bleisser wrote:

> *There is an expression, "funny as a crutch," which is used to suggest that there are some things that are so tragic that there is no room for humor. To say that there is nothing funny about a crutch may seem obvious; however, I can assure you that for those people who use crutches there is much they find that is funny about them.*[56]

My father told us younger children simple stories that he felt we could understand. He practiced the more complex stories on my mother and my adult sisters. When the stories were quite polished, he brought them out at parties. Even his simple stories sounded funny to us: the day he fell on the floor and found out he had polio; the time he watched an undertaker cut a jacket up the back because it was too difficult to put on a stiff body; how he was always asked as a young man to be a pallbearer because he was the strongest man in the neighborhood;

how he was afraid to sleep in his own bed as a child because both his grandfathers had died there.

His longer stories were directed at his adult children and I resented that. I only half listened to them. They had to do with small mishaps of his, not all polio-related.

One of them I witnessed. In 1964 we were at the New York World's Fair. To take one ride, we had to make our way to our seats across a sort of moving sidewalk. The sidewalk was one big circle surrounding seats also arranged in a circle. It was easy for my brothers to run across it and jump into a seat. It was more difficult for me. I was a tall, thin, awkward teenage girl with a curvature of the spine. I managed to make it over to my brothers and sit down. When I looked up, I saw my father trying to negotiate the moving sidewalk. He started to sway. Suddenly two men in suits "in suits!" he exclaimed later (no one in their right mind would be wearing suits at the World's Fair), grabbed him, stopped the ride and escorted him off.

In 1961 or 1962 he parked in a dentist's parking place. He had to meet with someone in a fancy restaurant and the sidewalks were icy. The dentist's parking place was the closest. After he had had a few drinks, some policemen came in and arrested him for illegal parking!! He was taken to the courthouse where he slipped and dislocated his elbow. A doctor came and said, "This will really hurt" and he yanked Dad's elbow back in place. Dad said later that it didn't hurt at all because of all the *anesthesia* he had at lunch. At some point he went before a judge and the dentist said, "I don't remember your name." He said, "Oh, it's a real hard one. It's J O O O N N E E S S S—Jones".

Once Arnold Bleisser and his wife went out to lunch. She left him for just a minute on a flat area on the top of a hill. His brakes gave way, and his chair started rolling down the hill. It picked up speed. There was nothing he could do because he was paralyzed in both arms and both legs. He claimed he wasn't afraid and began to enjoy the ride. The wheelchair finally crashed into a brand new sports car. He broke his leg. An ambulance took him to the nearest E.R. and when he finally got to see a doctor, he explained that he had a broken leg.

The doctor looked at his chart and said, "I see that you are a psychiatrist. I think I am a little depressed. Could you recommend an antidepressant?" Bleisser explained that his leg hurt. "Could we discuss this later?" But the doctor wouldn't let it go. Finally, Bleisser recommended one off the top of his head.

The doctor said, "Okay! Now we can get an X-ray of your leg." After he walked away, Bleisser started laughing and completely forgot the pain.[57]

When an orthopedist came to his home days later his pain was nearly gone and he was in an "inordinately good mood." He asked the doctor if he would be able to walk again when his leg was healed. The doctor said, "Of course." Bleisser started chuckling and said, "That's wonderful. I couldn't walk before."

Bleisser said, "He did not smile. He did not laugh. In fact, what I had said did not even seem to register as remotely funny. His seriousness only made me laugh harder. I'm sure he was convinced that my problem was less in my legs than in my head."[58]

Acceptance

It is important to learn to accept the tragic things that happen to you. Charles Mee said, "I learned to accept the world as it was and to adjust to it, that's the way I had been raised."[59]

Another polio survivor said, "If one were to say to me today that I could be rid of my polio on the condition that I would also be rid of everything that I have learned during the course of this disease, I would hesitate."

Jeane Dille said she's grateful for the love and support of her husband and for the fact that she lived to see her children reach adulthood. Polio helped her understand that "my children were my most precious gifts." She was also grateful that she could sing and get her doctoral degree.[60]

Georgina Bailey wrote an article entitled "I'm glad I had polio."[61]

A polio survivor living on a respirator said, "When it comes to the nitty-gritty, when it comes right down to it, you surprise yourself with wanting to live despite it all."[62]

Arnold Bleisser wrote:

> *Things happen that we do not want, that we fought against to keep from happening, things that were painful and disruptive. But they brought unexpected opportunities once they happened, and there was no way of turning back. In order to see the opportunities, though, you must accept what happened as if you had chosen it. Whatever comes next, I hope I will be able to remember that lesson.*[63]

4. FDR and the March of Dimes

And then he said, "You know President Roosevelt had polio." I could only think, how could he possibly think I don't know that?

—Anne Finger

Franklin Roosevelt, who had the enormous good luck of having an impressive last name, a sunny disposition and a handsome face and body, was able to easily obtain political office and appointments. Until, that is, he was struck with polio in 1921. He founded an important rehabilitation center in Warm Springs Georgia. In 1928 he was talked into running for governor of New York. Because of the Great Depression and because of his great comeback story from polio he won the presidency in 1932. In 1934 the "Birthday Balls" were started and managed to raise enough money to save Roosevelt's

Warm Springs rehabilitation center from bankruptcy and provide some money for research into polio. In 1938 F.D.R. established the National Foundation for Infantile Paralysis (NFIP) called the March of Dimes for short. The "Birthday Balls" were stopped. F.D.R. asked his friend Basil O'Connor to run the Foundation and it became the most successful charitable institution ever formed. It was run mostly by volunteers. People eagerly opened their wallets so that the NFIP could find a cure for this sad, sad disease. 80% of patients received financial aid from the NFIP. Also the NFIP gave grants to scientists who eventually came up with two popular polio vaccines.

Childhood, Youth and Young Adulthood

James Roosevelt met his second wife Sara Delano at the home of Mittie Roosevelt, the mother of future president Theodore Roosevelt, who was then at Harvard. James couldn't take his eyes off Sara. She was tall, dark-eyed with auburn hair and looked much like her future son Franklin.

Franklin Delano Roosevelt was born on January 30, 1882. He had a childhood anyone would envy: wealthy doting parents; home schooled by governesses; a father who taught him to swim, sail, fish and ride; a pony of his own; trips to Europe and at 16 he got a sailboat.

He liked stamp collecting and learned French well enough to converse with Charles de Gaulle during World War II. He liked memorizing interesting facts and was once caught studying the Webster's Unabridged dictionary.

When he was five he met a depressed and tired-looking President Cleveland. Cleveland put his hand on the child's head and said, "My little man, I am making a strange wish for you. It is that you may never be President of the United States."[1]

In September of 1896 he was sent to Groton, an upper-class boarding school in Massachusetts. Because of his sheltered childhood he didn't know how to get along with other boys but was so charming that no one picked on him.[2]

As a teenager, his distant cousins called him "Feather Duster" for his initials FD. Alice Roosevelt, Theodore's daughter, called him "Miss Nancy" a euphemism for homosexual. At Harvard students were irritated by his eagerness to please and didn't accept him into the exclusive Porcellain club.

At Harvard he became editor of the *Crimson*. He did not fit in with the other boys there. "He was never one of the boys although he frequently made a good try," a secret service agent said later. His secretary said he "was really incapable of a personal friendship with anyone."[3]

His father died of heart disease when Franklin was in his freshman year at Harvard. His mother remarked that Theodore Roosevelt's father also had died while he was in freshman year at Harvard. They felt that this was a good omen. Because Theodore was his hero, Franklin made politics his chosen field.

Franklin took his mother to Europe to ease her sadness over her husband's death. While in France they heard that President William McKinley had been shot. When they landed in New York they learned that Theodore Roosevelt was now president. Franklin seemed to be following in the footsteps of Theodore. Like Theodore, he served in the New York State Assembly, became Assistant Secretary of the Navy, ran for Vice President, became Governor of New York and President of the United States.[4]

In 1902 Franklin ran into Eleanor Roosevelt who had been at school in England. She was fashionably dressed, had a good figure, long upswept blond hair and large eyes.[5] They quickly fell in love but postponed marriage for his mother's sake. They got married on March 17, 1905. The President gave her away and after the ceremony said, "Well, Franklin, there's nothing like keeping the name in the family."[6] They had five children who survived infancy.

Early Career

Franklin worked as a lawyer and later became a New York State Senator.

At the 1912 Democratic National Convention in Baltimore, Maryland, he met and became friends with Josephus Daniels. When Wilson won the presidency, Daniels was asked to be the Secretary of the Navy. Remembering the charming Franklin D. Roosevelt, Daniels asked him to become the Assistant Secretary of the Navy. In 1920 Roosevelt was nominated to run for vice president under Governor James M. Cox of Ohio. Cox was badly beaten by Warren G. Harding.[7]

Franklin was well-liked but his desire to please everyone could wear on them. Although he was not effeminate, he was not a man's man and people wondered if he could take the rough-and-tumble world of politics. Everything had come too easy for him. He was named to Wilson's cabinet with little effort on his part and stumbled into the 1920 vice presidential nomination the same way.[8]

He tried to follow Theodore Roosevelt's path to the presidency. It was quite a coup when he married the president's favorite niece, Eleanor. Now he could call President Roosevelt "Uncle Ted." [9]

Franklin's Illness

President Franklin Delano Roosevelt may not have had polio. He may have had Guillain-Barre syndrome (GBS). That disease begins in the feet, advances up the body and can cut off breathing. It includes loss of feeling. In polio there is no loss of feeling.[10] His slowly and symmetrically ascending paralysis, his severe pain and hypersensitivity can also occur in polio but is more common in GBS. His unusual symptoms may have been why his doctors were so confused. Also, usually only children got polio at that time. A lumbar puncture was not done right away so we will never know.

The disease was named in 1916 after French physicians Georges Guillain and Jean Alexandre Barre. It is usually triggered by an infection and except for accidents it is the most common cause of paralysis. Unlike some diseases it does not affect the brain or spinal cord.

The important thing is that he *thought* he had polio. Everyone *thought* he had polio and as president he was able to mobilize the country against the disease.

Franklin had always been sickly. He had had scarlet fever, typhoid, measles, mumps, sinus infections, colds, lumbago, hives, throat infections and double pneumonia. He had always been home schooled and had been exposed to very few children. He had not had a chance to build up immunity to their diseases.[11]

In 1921 he was under stress because of a two-year-old scandal at the naval training station at Newport, Rhode Island. In 1919 he had authorized an investigation of homosexual liaisons which had included using sailers to entrap other sailers.[12]

That same year, on his way to his summer home of Campobello, he stopped at a Boy Scout camp which had unsanitary conditions. Toilets overflowed. There was no way to wash your hands and the drinking water was polluted with fecal matter, known to cause polio. There is a high probability that he caught his disease there.[13]

By the time he got to Campobello he felt drained, but he sailed, fought a brush fire, jogged, swam across a stream and swam in the ocean. He later sat down to look at his mail, too tired to change out of his swim suit. His lower back ached. He skipped dinner and went to bed. The next morning he had stabbing pains in his back, ached all over and had a fever.[14]

He was in great pain. If he had polio, it felt like nails were being hammered into his flesh or his teeth were being drilled without anesthesia. Often people have hallucinations and nightmares. He found he was too weak to hold a pencil and he could not stand.[15]

The doctors were puzzled. Adults did not usually get polio in 1921. The disease became more virulent in the 1930s, 40s and 50s and at that time was able to overcome an adult's immunity to the disease. The doctors may not even have considered polio. A lumbar puncture was recommended in the first 24 hours which would have confirmed that it was polio and would have relieved pressure in his spine but it was not done.

Meanwhile, Eleanor took charge of the unpleasant task of nursing him. He was helpless as a baby. He had to be fed, lifted, his body had to be moved to make him more comfortable, she had to help him relieve his bowels and bladder and bathe him. She later said, "In all our contacts it is probably the sense of being really needed which gives the greatest satisfaction and creates the most lasting bond."[16]

After a few weeks, someone called Dr. Robert Lovett, one of the three directors of the Harvard Infantile Paralysis Commission and convinced him to come to Campobello.

Dr. Lovett was a 61-year-old orthopedist who worked with physiotherapists, a new profession which helped soldiers wounded in World War I.

When he examined Franklin he found that his breathing was good, he was sensitive to the touch, his bladder was not infected even though he was using a catheter, his arms were weak and his abdominal muscles were normal. Also he had atrophy in the ball of his left thumb and marked weakness in his hips.

When Lovett gave his diagnosis—polio—Franklin looked horrified. Eleanor would see that same expression 20 years later when he was told about the bombing of Pearl Harbor.[17]

Dr. Lovett tried to give the family some hope. He told them exercise would help and that muscles could spontaneously recover. It was a "mild case" and "complete or partial recovery was possible." He reassured them that the children may have gotten it but had fought it off. He advised them to hire a trained nurse. But he privately admitted that any improvement "would be very slight."[18]

Franklin's mother was on a cruise and they did not want to bother her with the bad news. She was met at the pier by her brother and told then. She immediately went to Campobello and found everyone determined to be cheerful. "I hear them all laughing," she wrote, "Eleanor in the lead."

She continued:

> *Below his waist he cannot move at all. His legs (that I have always been so proud of) have to be moved often as they ache when long in one position....They have no power.*

His personal physician, Dr. Draper, believed the patient's state of mind affected the outcome of his disease. Knowing that Franklin read newspapers, he told reporters that Roosevelt was "temporarily unable to walk." It was, he said, "a mild case." And, he was "already regaining use off his legs."[19]

At Campobello, he regained control of his bladder and bowels. Then he was sent to a hospital where he told everybody he was going to be fine. Still, he had pain and abnormal sensitivity to touch. The doctor found that his body was completely useless below the waist but he had strength in his back muscles and could sit up. As long as he had pain he was to rest but he should sit up in a chair for one hour a day. At the end of October the pain was gone.[20]

He tried to remain cheerful. He wrote, "The doctors say, however, that my progress is excellent and even more rapid than they had hoped." Yet he must have been mourning all he had lost and felt that he must have done something bad to deserve this.[21]

Eleanor wanted him to keep following politics. But she never expected him to hold another political office. When Dr. Draper said he was well enough to resume normal activities, he claimed that he would walk again and no one was allowed to tell him otherwise.

Like most victims of polio, Franklin became angry. He was angry at everyone who had underestimated him. Everyone who called him a momma's boy, a prig, "Miss Nancy," "Feather Duster." Didn't they know he was aware of what they were saying? He was furious at the Porcellians at Harvard, the exclusive club that had black balled him. At his mother who wanted him to retire to Hyde Park. And at polio. Polio would keep him out of politics for so very long. In spite of everyone who had ever tried to hold him back, he was determined to achieve his dream.[22]

By December of 1921, his legs had been motionless for four months. Mrs. Kathleen Lake, a physiotherapist, evaluated him. His arms, stomach and lower back were strong. She had him do pull-ups. And eventually his upper body became very powerful.[23]

When Franklin Roosevelt ran for vice president in 1920, Al Smith ran for governor of New York and was narrowly defeated. In 1922 Al Smith ran for governor again and won.

Meanwhile, Roosevelt was gaining strength. Dr. Lovett tried to convince him to use crutches and wrote it was "an art, acquired by constant practice," keep at it.

Franklin did but made little progress probably because his pelvic muscles were so weak.[24]

In an effort to recuperate, Franklin rented a houseboat and sailed around the Florida Keys. He came back looking healthier and able to hold his right knee in a fixed position.[25]

He took up new hobbies and renewed old ones. He built model sailboats for racing, bought farmland in Hyde Park and planted trees there, worked on the Roosevelt family genealogy, became Hyde Park village's official historian, went back to collecting rare books and stamps, read American History and wrote to Democrats all over the country.[26]

In the fall of 1923 he bought a houseboat for a cruise he was planning in early 1924. [27]

Al Smith

His friend, Al Smith, figured that if he could get the Democratic nomination for president in 1924, he would lose, but would have a good chance of running again in 1928. He asked Franklin to give the speech nominating him to run as president. Franklin and his son Jimmy measured how far Franklin would have to walk on crutches to get to the lectern. It was 20 feet. They practiced it over and over. When the day came, he grabbed Jimmy's hand and then let go of it, walking by himself to the lectern. "He was terribly crippled," Frances Perkins, Secretary of Labor from 1933 to 1945, said, but he reached the lectern. Women wept. "It just tore the place to pieces," Perkins said. "His voice was strong and true and vigorous."

The crowd cheered for over an hour. He had called Al Smith "the happy warrior," "the man of destiny." Later these words would be used to describe him.[28]

Years later, people said they had seen a ray of light come through the skylight and shine on his head.

The Louisville Courier-Journal said, "Franklin D. Roosevelt showed that this was the stuff he was made of." Some people suggested that Roosevelt take the nomination.[29]

Smith lost the Democratic nomination. He ran for governor and was reelected. He began to plan for 1928.

Basil O'Connor

Franklin became friendly with lawyer Basil O'Connor when he slipped and fell in the building where they worked. O'Connor heard him call out, "Nothing to worry about!" O'Connor and another man helped him up. Then Roosevelt said, "Let's go."

Unlike Roosevelt, O'Connor was not from a rich family. He was, he would say, "just two generations away from Irish servitude." Against O'Connor's better judgement, he became Roosevelt's partner in buying the dilapidated Warm Springs, Georgia health spa.[30] Roosevelt had bought Warm Springs in 1926 and in 1945 he died there. He made a total of fifty visits, some of them lasting for months.[31]

Warm Springs, Georgia had natural springs which were very warm—-90 degrees Fahrenheit. The Springs were in Bullochville, Georgia, the home of Eleanor's grandmother Mittie Bulloch Roosevelt. When Franklin first laid eyes on it the resort was empty and run down. The swimming pool was 89 degrees Fahrenheit and four feet deep. Franklin got in and stood. He walked.

Franklin loved the warm water that was buoyant enough to let him stand. He invited polio victims to use it for therapy. Some came uninvited. Roosevelt sized them up and developed a method for testing muscle function. Basil O'Connor incorporated the nonprofit Warm Springs Foundation with the intention of doing something about polio.[32] The conquest of polio later became a national crusade. [33]

Patients were able to exercise in the buoyant water for hours without tiring. Dr. Frank Dickenson visited and said the water treatment was "effective" and "not overtaxing." The patients mental attitude and their physical strength was much improved. The water was great for "muscle training therapy."[34]

By 1926 Roosevelt had come to realize that his future did not include walking. But he could work, conduct meetings, make speeches, persuade and charm. To succeed politically his walking needed to appear more natural. He hired Alice Lou Plastridge, a physiotherapist. Her goal was to make his walking more inconspicuous and quiet. She showed him how to use his upper body to help move his legs. He went to Warm Springs to practice what she had taught him and learned to walk with two canes, no crutches and no arm to cling to.[35]

By 1928 he was spending time raising money for improvements to Warm Springs and to pay off the mortgage.[36]

Governor of New York

In 1928 Al Smith wanted him to run for governor of New York while Smith ran for president. Franklin was still practicing walking. He could walk with one hand grasping a boy's hand and one hand on a cane. His gait was smooth and slow, almost natural. One day he even walked across a room with only his braces on. He wanted to spend two more years perfecting this. He did not want to run for governor. [37]

Smith was insistent. Why couldn't he run? His walking was fine and he had a magnificent voice. And there was that Roosevelt name. Roosevelt didn't think he or Smith had a chance of winning. Smith secretly thought Roosevelt's health wouldn't allow him to perform the duties of governor. Smith met with other Democrats and the name Roosevelt kept coming up. So they checked with Eleanor. "Was Franklin's health good enough to be governor?" It was, she replied, but he would have to go back and forth to Warm Springs for treatment.

Finally Smith telephoned Franklin and asked him point blank to run. He said he could spend most of his time at Warm Springs.

"Don't hand me that baloney," Roosevelt said. Then Smith said he needed him to run. If New York had a Democratic governor, Smith could hold New York in the election. To stay on Smith's and the Democrats good side, Franklin knew he would have to run.[38]

If by some miracle he was elected governor, he had a good chance at the White House later.

When asked how a person who could not even walk on his own could be governor, he said, "After all, muscular weakness in one's legs had nothing whatever to do with the vigor and endurance of one's mind."

Smith whose language was more colorful said:

> *A governor does not have to be an acrobat. We do not elect him for his ability to do a double backflip or a handspring. The work of the governorship is brainwork [and] there is no doubt of [Franklin Roosevelt's] ability to do it.*

He travelled by auto caravan across New York. He would move slowly with one hand on a cane and the other on a man's arm. "I am on my feet," he would state, "and entirely capable, at least from the physical point of view, of running any business, whether a private business or that of the government of the state of New York!"

Smith lost to Hoover who won in a landslide and he lost New York. Roosevelt won—just barely.[39]

Roosevelt was now governor of the most populous state in the union. If he proved his executive ability there he had a good chance of winning the White House later.

If the economy remained strong, Hoover would win a second term in 1932. But in 1936 Roosevelt fully intended to try for the presidency. His comeback from polio would help him.

As a polio survivor he needed to be left alone and figure out what he could do on his own. Al Smith continually tried to advise him. Perkins tried to explain that there comes a time in every person's life when they have to break free of their mother, for example. Smith did not understand. He had the perfect mother. She was always right. He always followed her advice. He became so resentful of the fact he couldn't control the governor that he refused to endorse him for president later.[40]

In 1930 Franklin won the governorship by an impressive margin—the largest ever seen in New York. Because of the stock market crash of 1929 Herbert Hoover was vulnerable. The Republicans were blamed for the Great Depression.

Journalist Russel Baker was told:

> Men were killing themselves because of Herbert Hoover, and their fatherless children were being packed away to orphanages because of Herbert Hoover.

1 in 4 workers had lost their jobs. Stocks had lost 80% of their value. Banks closed.

President

Franklin Roosevelt ran for president in 1932. His physical disability would be brought up many times during the race for president but, as his son said, "After all, it's a desk job."[41]

Without polio he would have been, as Walter Lippman put it, "a pleasant man who…would very much like to be president." Polio kept him out of politics during the mid-1920s when Democrats had no hope of succeeding.

It kept him out until 1928 when he was well enough to run for governor. In 1928 he discovered that he was able to run for an office without being able to walk. And polio gave him a great comeback story.

Perkins said polio had changed him. When she saw him in 1924 she said, "I was instantly struck by his growth.... He was serious, not playing now...He was not born great, but became great." Many noticed his extraordinary character and his deep affection for people.[42]

National Foundation for Infantile Paralysis

He still was interested in keeping Warm Springs going.

On January 30, 1934 Franklin Roosevelt's 52nd birthday, Basil O'Connor began the annual Birthday Balls held across the nation. The motto was "Dance so that others can walk." Over one million dollars were raised to pay off debts at the Warm Springs resort and enough money remained to start the funding of research projects.

In 1938 F.D.R. founded the National Foundation for Infantile Paralysis (NFIP). Since Roosevelt was otherwise occupied, O'Connor was chosen to head it. The Birthday Balls were discontinued. The headquarters for the NFIP were located at O'Connor's law firm at 120 Broadway in New York.[43]

There were 3,000 local chapters with 90,000 year-round volunteers. There were 5 paid regional directors who reported to National Headquarters. 2,000,000 other volunteers worked during the January fund drives. The money was sent to National Headquarters to be distributed from there.[44] One half of the money raised would go to polio victims in the area. All major decisions such as who to award grants to would be made by National Headquarters.[45]

Eddie Cantor, the comedy star, suggested the name "March of Dimes" after a popular newsreel called the "March of Time." He asked radio personalities to use their programs to ask for contributions. He also asked everyone to send a dime to the White House. 1.8 million dollars was collected, 268,000 in dimes. The Lone Ranger, Jack Benny, Humphrey Bogart, Jimmy Cagney and Kate Smith advertised for the March of Dimes on the air. Short films starring Judy Garland, Mickey Rooney, Jimmy Stewart and Robert Young were played in movie theaters before the main feature. Money would be collected by ushers after the short polio films.[46]

The NFIP became "the most successful public fundraising campaign of all time." It portrayed polio as America's enemy and people were urged to give anything they could afford, no matter how small, to the charity. Every January the March of Dimes collected money door to door. By December of 1941 they were collecting 3 million each year.[47] The NFIP played on the American people's fear that their children would become crippled by polio. The NFIP became so successful that there was never any need to provide public assistance for polio victims.[48] Newspaper editors complained that there was more money raised for polio than for cancer, heart disease and TB combined even though these diseases had higher death rates.[49]

It was a volunteer-based organization and there was no shortage of volunteers to fight a disease that crippled thousands of children every year.

Greater than 80% of the polio patients received aid.[50] The NFIP's guidelines were to give financial aid to "any family which would have to lower its standard of living by paying the total costs of medical and hospital care."[51] In severe cases they paid for home care and encouraged the family to help with the required physical therapy. [52]

In 1944 the organization helped my father become the first man to be admitted to the excellent Children's Hospital-School in Baltimore, Maryland. The local NFIP chapter visited a patient as soon as they heard that he had polio and found out how much financial support he would need.

The NFIP also paid for patients hospital costs, iron lungs, rocking beds, hydrotherapy, braces, wheelchairs and household help. The chapters dispensed the money and moved nurses, physical therapists and equipment to areas with epidemics.[53] Between 1938 and 1955 ten times as much money was spent on patient care as on research.[54]

In the 1950s so much was spent on patient care that the ability to continue research on preventing polio was threatened. In 1954 the 54 million raised in January was not enough so there was an emergency drive in August.[55]

The first poster child, six-year-old Donald Anderson, appeared in 1944. The poster showed before and after treatment pictures. The before pictures showed him in a crib looking miserable, the after showed him walking jauntily. No mention was made of the back brace he had to wear for the rest of his life. The implication was that the boy, close to death, had been brought back to health by contributions to the March of Dimes.[56] From that time on, individual chapters selected a poster child of their own.

In 1949, after three years in an iron lung at Baltimore's Children's Hospital-School, a picture was taken of Carolyn S. age 18. It shows her writing with her mouth, "I am helping the polio epidemic drive. Are you?"[57]

In the late 1940s one March of Dimes chapter had housewives go door to door to collect contributions. The slogan was "Turn on your Porch Light! Help Fight Polio Tonight." They collected an average of one dollar per family. In 1951 the NFIP organized a nationwide Mother's March. They raised 250 million in the 1950s partly because of the excitement over the coming vaccine.[58]

Shortly before he died FDR said:

The fight being waged against infantile paralysis...is an essential part of the struggle in which we are all engaged. Nothing is closer to my heart than the health of our boys and girls and young men and women. To me it is one of the front lines of our national defense.[59]

Dad Volunteers to Work for the NFIP

Dad volunteered to work for the NFIP, eventually becoming chairman of the Baltimore Chapter. He was a member of the Ortho Club which went into rural areas to ask for money. He also served on the March of Dimes speakers committee. The NFIP tried to get speakers who had had polio and were successful at their jobs or speakers whose children had had polio. A speaker would show a picture of their paralyzed child in bed and at the end of the speech introduce the happy child getting around on crutches paid for by the NFIP. Sometimes speakers would show a film such as the one starring Helen Hayes whose daughter had died of polio. Speakers always mentioned new discoveries into the prevention of polio and said that the research was paid for by the March of Dimes. Dad would emphasize that this disease can happen to anyone. He also outlined the work of the National Foundation. He spoke from his heart as only a polio survivor could. Like most polio victims the speakers complained about people trying to help them do things they could easily do for themselves. "I have the hardest time convincing my firm that I do not need help in my job—that I can handle it," Dad said. Another speaker said, "We helped do war work, and can help ourselves now. People are looking on the handicapped in a different way and are giving us a chance."[60]

In 1952 the Corporations and Business committee of the 1953 March of Dimes increased its financial goal. Since Dad was partner with his brother in a food brokerage firm he was named head of the food committee and lobbied grocery stores for contributions to the March of Dimes. He continued in this position for many years. Since he was president of the Maryland Food Brokers Association and secretary of the Grocers Manufacturers Representatives Association of Baltimore he had many contacts in this area.

Other committees were advertising, architect, automobile, bakeries, breweries, business equipment, chemical, men's retail clothing, specialty shops, clothing, dairies, contractors, electrical, engineers, financial institutions, fuel, home furnishings, hotels, ice cream, insurance, jewelry, laundry, liquors, lumber, metal and glass, miscellaneous, manufacturers, paper, printing, real estate, retail merchants, soap, soft drinks and dental.

The committee heads were told to raise twice as much money as they had in 1952, the worst year of the epidemic.[61]

In 1954 Dad was chosen to be secretary of the Baltimore city chapter of the NFIP. In August of that year he was appointed chairman of the Business and Labor committee for the emergency March of Dimes. The emergency drive was necessary, he said, "because not enough money was raised in the January drive to provide both for patients and polio prevention during 1954."

August, 1954
JONES HEADS POLIO GROUP

Named To Post For Emergency March of Dimes

H. Edwin Jones, a Baltimore business man who is himself a victim of polio, has been appointed chairman of the Business and Labor Committee for the Emergency March of Dimes, it was announced yesterday.

Earl R. Lewis, chairman of the emergency drive, said that the first organizing meeting of the committee would be held at 12:15 P.M. on Thursday in the Park Plaza Hotel.

There plans will be discussed for the drive, which will be held on August 16 through August 31.

Mr. Jones said that, as in the past, business and labor organizations in Baltimore "have given the most gratifying support" to the March of Dimes.

"Is Imperative Now"

He said that they would not let the polio sufferers of the nation down at a time when the search for improved preventive and treatment techniques must be continued if a victory over the disease is to be won.

"The Emergency March of Dimes is imperative now because not enough money was raised in the January drive to provide both for patients and polio prevention during 1954," he said.

Mr. Jones, who has been working for the March of Dimes for ten years, was the first man with polio to be admitted to the Children's Hospital for treatment.

He lost the use of both legs when he was afflicted with polio in 1944, but is still actively engaged in the wholesale food business, and is past president of the Maryland Food Brokers' Association.[62]

In April of 1955 he was once again elected secretary of the Baltimore chapter.

In 1956 he became a member of the advisory board for the 1956 March of Dimes and a member of the National Foundation's executive committee.

In April of 1956 he was elected chairman of the Baltimore chapter.

April, 1956
Former Victim Of Polio Will Head Unit

H. Edwin Jones, Baltimore business man and a victim of polio, has been elected chairman of the Baltimore chapter of the National Foundation for Infantile Paralysis.

Other chapter officers for 1956-1957 include Mrs. Ellsworth Armacost, first vice president; Walter Komorowski, second vice president; Earl R. Lewis, third vice president; T. Read Fulton, treasurer; Mrs. Maurice Roycroft, assistant treasurer, and C. Warren Colgan, secretary.

Edmund G. Garbee and J. Neil McCardell have been elected to the chapter's executive committee.

Stricken with polio in 1944, Mr. Jones has been active in March of Dimes campaigns for the last ten years. It was through the help of the National Foundation that he became the first man with poliomyelitis to be admitted to the Children's Hospital for treatment.

Earlier Posts

Mr. Jones has served on March of Dimes speakers' committee, has been chairman of the food committee of the Business and Labor division of campaigns since 1951, and in August, 1954, was chairman of the Business and Labor division for the Emergency March of Dimes drive.

In addition, he was a member of the advisory board for the 1956 March of Dimes and has been a member of the National Foundation's executive committee in Baltimore since 1953.

Although he lost the use of both legs when polio struck, Mr. Jones is actively engaged in the wholesale food business.[63]

In 1957 he was still giving talks on polio. He also appeared on a live television show called *Comeback!* We all gathered around the TV to watch it. All I remember about it was a great deal was made of him having had three children after he was struck with polio. At 7-years-old I couldn't understand what the fuss was all about.

After working ten years for the National Foundation my father received a certificate from Basil O'Connor:

Certificate of Appreciation

Fight
Infantile
Paralysis

THIS EXPRESSION OF ESTEEM IS
AWARDED TO H. EDWIN JONES
for ten years of outstanding service in the
fight against Infantile Paralysis, not only for
devoted efforts toward increasing Chapter
accomplishments but also for the added
scientific Knowledge such efforts have helped
make possible

May 24, 1956

Basil O'Connor
PRESIDENT
THE NATIONAL FOUNDATION FOR
INFANTILE PARALYSIS
FRANKLIN D. ROOSEVELT, FOUNDER

Patients Praise March of Dimes

Margy H. said that the "March of Dimes totally covered the cost of my treatment."[64]

Ronny D. said that six months of her hospital stay was paid for.[65]

Susan P. whose father died of polio in 1952 when she was nine said, "I know the March of Dimes helped a lot with all the hospital expenses."[66]

Kathy H., born August 1, 1948 got polio in September of 1949 and stayed in the hospital for four years. She walked out of the hospital on braces and crutches. She said, "I believe the March of Dimes helped out with all my medical expenses....What a gift the March of Dimes was for families like ours."[67]

The March of Dimes paid for Katalin W.'s treatment.[68]

Jeane Dille found the March of Dimes "awe-inspiring" and remarked on "how much I owed and still owe to this marvelous organization." The March of Dimes paid her hospitalization, nurses, surgeries, iron lung and physical therapy. It also paid for all the additional rehabilitation and surgery she has had over the years.[69]

Shriners hospitals helped also. The hospital administrator handed Jim J.'s father a bill for Jim's treatment. His father start to explain that he would have to take out a second mortgage on his house to pay it. The man said, "Mr. J., read it again." At the bottom of the invoice it said, "Paid in full, a gift from the Shriners."[70]

Money was also given to Jonas Salk in Pittsburgh who was working on a vaccine.

5. The Vaccine

*One must work, one must work. I have done
what I could.—*

Louis Pasteur's last words

*Because of two failed attempts to create polio vaccines
in 1935, time wasted trying to prove false theories of
what causes the disease, money needed to fight World
War II, and money needed for patient care, work on a
polio vaccine was postponed until 1947.*

*There was thought to be three types of polio. This had
to be verified. Also there were many strains of polio.
Scientists had to figure out what strains were contained
in what types. This job, called typing would be sheer
drudgery. It could be done by "anyone." The job was
given to four separate labs around the country. Jonas
Salk recognized that it was an important step in creating
a polio vaccine which would prevent his children's generation and future generations from getting polio. He
became the spokesman for the typing project.[1]*

*Salk's lab was the first one to complete the typing proj-
ect and the first one to use John Ender's discovery that
poliovirus could be grown in non-nervous tissue culture.
He won many awards after his vaccine came out but he
said it wasn't the awards that count:*

It is not the awards made by men that give us the greatest reason for doing. The real reason is known to each and every one of us. Those who have experienced the feeling that comes with finding out what they set out to learn or of discovering something they didn't expect, have enjoyed the satisfaction of a moment that could never again be exceeded but could be equaled if they could do more....[2]

• • •

Milkmaids had tried, time and again, to tell doctors that they became immune from smallpox after getting cowpox. Cowpox caused ugly sores on their hands but the sores went away after three weeks. Using pus from an infected milkmaid, Edward Jenner infected a little boy with cowpox. The boy developed a mild case of smallpox and then recovered. Afterwards, at risk children were regularly infected with cowpox in order to prevent a deadly case of smallpox.[3]

Unfortunately rarely does something as benign as cowpox exist in animals for other deadly diseases. Scientists had to work in the laboratory to develop vaccines. Typhoid, cholera and plague bacteria were killed in the laboratory by using heat or deadly chemicals, leaving enough fragments to stimulate antibodies that would attack the original virus. The tuberculosis vaccine was a live but weakened or attenuated vaccine. Bovine tuberculosis bacterium from an infected heifer was pushed through potato, glycerine and ox bile. The TB vaccine has been in use since 1927.[4] The poliovirus was *killed* by mixing it with formalin and *weakened* by pushing it through several monkeys.

In 1885 Louis Pasteur became a hero when he gave his rabies shots to a nine-year-old boy who had been bitten by a rabid dog. He saved the boy's life.

In 1929 Carl Kling proved that polio went to the intestines. He was ignored by the scientific community.

In 1941 Albert Sabin found polio virus in the walls of the intestines proving that that is how it got into the human body. Sabin began to consider the possibility of creating an oral vaccine.[5]

Simon Flexnor discovered in 1899 one of the main causes of bacillary dysentery and created a meningitis antiserum used for over thirty years. He headed the Rockefeller Institute and edited the *Journal of Experimental Medicine*. He ruled the Rockefeller with an iron hand. In 1935 he stopped all investigation into a polio vaccine when a dangerous vaccine killed several children. Scientists wasted years trying to prove his theory that polio enters through the nose. (It enters through the mouth.) He also believed there was only one type of polio virus when there are three. [6]

In 1935 Dr. Maurice Brodie tested his vaccine on hundreds of children. The vaccine was ineffective and could cause severe allergic reactions. Because of this, he lost his job at the New York University School of Medicine.[7] In the same year, Dr. John Kolmer of Philadelphia gave live polio vaccine to thousands of children. 6 died and 3 were paralyzed. None developed immunity to polio.[8]

People assumed that both vaccines were backed by the yearly birthday balls.

Kolmer died honored for his role in eradicating diphtheria. Brodie, who was much younger than Kolmer, and whose career was ruined, died at age 36 probably of suicide.[9]

The development of a vaccination against polio was forbidden until as late as 1947.

Tom Rivers

Tom Rivers, a short and stocky rough neck from the South with "a voice like a bullfrog,"[10] was dismayed that so many Jews were becoming powerful in his field of virology. To him everyone was a boy "an old boy, a smart boy, a good old boy, or a Jew boy." But he recognized talent and recruited the cream of the crop for which Basil O'Connor was grateful.[11] He had gotten his MD from Johns Hopkins in 1916. He had trained as a pediatrician but decided to work in lab research. He worked at the Rockefeller Institute for virus research in the United States. The first generation of virologists were trained in his lab.[12]

He said of O'Connor, "That old man didn't know anymore about science than my left shoe but he was willing to learn." O'Connor said of him, "He was extremely learned but not what you'd call exceedingly bright."[13]

When Albert Sabin came back after spending a year in England, Rivers noticed that he was wearing tweeds and spats, smoking a pipe and carrying a cane. "God damn you, Sabin!" he said. "You can't turn a cheap East Side Jew into an Englishman in one year! Don't you ever come to see me with spats on again. Don't you ever speak to me in that broad accent again." Retelling the story he'd say, "You know, by God, he went back to being an East Side Jew, and he's been all right ever since."[14]

Dr. Harry Weaver appointed Director of research in 1946 said, "Old Tom Rivers acted as if I were a foreign agent during my first two years around the Foundation. He challenged everything I said. If I had said he was good-looking, he would have argued with me."[15]

Albert Sabin, Jonas Salk and Hilary Koprowski developed vaccines against polio. All happened to be Jewish.[16] So was John Enders who discovered that poliovirus could be grown in non-nervous tissue culture.

In 1949, the Surgeon General said to expect "the worst year for infantile paralysis in the history of the USA."[17] People in their twenties and thirties were also at risk and the chances of serious paralysis rose with age. 1949 was the worst year on record so far with 42,000 cases. The NFIP wanted to get rid of polio as soon as possible.[18]

In 1931 it was reported that there were only three types of the polio virus and in 1949 Jonas Salk was attempting to prove that fact by doing mind-numbing testing on monkeys.[19]

In the meantime, Hilary Koprowski was quietly working on an attenuated oral vaccine.

Hilary Koprowski

Koprowski was born in Poland on December 5, 1916. He created the first effective polio vaccine. His son said, "He was colorful, charismatic....He's still the most brilliant person I've ever met."[20]

He spoke Russian, Polish, French, Italian, English and Latin.[21] He was a renaissance man and was familiar with Shakespeare, all the sciences, music, history and world literature.

Once, he discussed fifteenth century Japanese poetry with some Japanese scientists. They were astounded to find out that he knew more about the subject than they did. He was a good writer and had an interesting conversational way of giving speeches. He was gracious, charming and self-assertive. It was difficult to say no to him. He could work on many things at one time. He worked on hog cholera virus, Japanese B encephalitis, Colorado tick fever and polio all in the same time frame.[22] He was also a good piano player and would have been a great one if he had had enough time to practice.[23]

His childhood was filled with books and music. The family was always listening to classical music on their gramophones. He took piano lessons at age 5 but felt he wasn't taught properly. He learned much more at age 12 when he went to the Warsaw Conservatory.

Because he was only fourth in his class, he chose to study medicine instead.

The Nazis occupied Warsaw in 1939. He, his wife, mother and father obtained visas to Brazil in 1940.[24]

He taught piano in Brazil until he ran into a former classmate who helped him get a job at the Rockefeller

Foundation in Rio. The interviewer noticed he had a very quick mind.

At the Rockefeller, yellow fever was the priority. Monkeys and mosquitos spread it to humans and the current vaccine had bad side effects. Yellow fever causes liver failure and kills one in every four people who get it.[25] With two other men he made a safe and effective vaccine for yellow fever. Scientists there also discovered that one virus can inhibit the growth of another virus. This was called interferon later.

He and his wife reluctantly left their friends in their Polish speaking community on December 1, 1944. Koprowski had been offered a job at Lederle Laboratories in New York.[26] Lederle synthesized vitamin B in 1947 and discovered aureomycin the antibiotic used for pneumonia.[27]

The lab director at Lederle was Herald Cox. He had not wanted the job. The place was much too high pressured for him. He demanded an outrageous salary hoping they would look elsewhere. They didn't. He put Koprowski to work on polio then had to leave several times for treatment of mental illness. [28]

Koprowski made a type II oral polio vaccine which he successfully tested on monkeys. On February 27, 1948 he tested his vaccine on 17 children at Letchworth Village, an institution for feeble-minded and epileptic children. They all developed antibodies to polio.

Koprowski spoke about his testing in Hershey, Pennsylvania at a Round Table Conference on Immunization in Poliomyelitis in March of 1951. The attendees had just had a big lunch and were starting to nod off. While he was talking Thomas Francis woke up and said, "What? Monkeys?" Salk said, "No. Children." Sabin yelled,

"How dare you feed live polio virus to children!" All hell broke loose. But less than a year later, Sabin was working on his own live vaccine and tried to test it on children. He was unable to obtain permission, so he resorted to testing it on prisoners.[29]

Koprowski said, "If we did such a thing now, Norton, Jervis, and I would be in jail and the company would be sued. If Jenner or Pasteur or Theiler or myself had to repeat and test our past discoveries in the 1990s, there would be no smallpox vaccine, no rabies vaccines, no yellow fever vaccine, and no live oral polio vaccine."[30]

Because he was commercially backed by Lederle and because of the uproar in Hershey, his findings were largely ignored by the NFIP. But he immediately began work on a Type I vaccine.[31]

He tested his new Type I and Type II oral live vaccine on the Sonoma State Home for the retarded. Parents gladly gave permission for the test.[32]

He tested it again in early 1958 in the Belgian Congo. A trial was going full swing in his native Poland when the announcement came that the Sabin vaccine was "suitable for use in the United States."[33]

It would have crushed a lesser man. Koprowski was the first scientist to invent a safe and effective polio vaccine. Not only that, a live oral vaccine was considered more effective than Salk's killed vaccine. But Koprowski claimed he was glad he was not turned into a celebrity. Celebrity wasted almost 3 decades of the lives of Salk and Sabin. Non-celebrity gave him the chance to "continue my scientific work undisturbed."[34]

Scientists under him produced a rubella vaccine. In 1968 he patented the rabies HDCV (human diploid cell vaccine). In 1975 45 people were bitten by dogs and wolves. The vaccine was used on them and was 100% effective. [35]

In the 1970s his group did work on early detection of cancer. [36] In 1983 they developed a rabies vaccine bait for raccoons, foxes and other wild animals.[37] He was given permission to test it on animals on an uninhabited island in Virginia.

At 75 he began to study composition and set poems to music. He also tested a contraceptive on the local deer population who had lost their natural habitat, were eating people's gardens and overpopulating the area. He still had 5 labs, took piano lessons, wrote scientific papers, fiction and plays. [38]

When he was almost 80, he had an adhesion of the bowel and had to have surgery. During his long recovery he decided to dictate his will in Latin. His son was "so envious of his IQ." He didn't think his father had spoken or read Latin in years. Koprowski said of this later, "Why did he tell that story? You don't die from bowel adhesion."[39]

At 80, he had a personal trainer and did stretching, calisthenics and swimming.[40] He looked younger than ever and was full of energy. One friend accused him of being immortal. He took music lessons, bought art, traveled, wrote letters and had discussions with colleagues.[41] At the Jefferson University he became professor in the microbiology and immunology department. One project was to find the cause of Multiple Sclerosis (MS) and to add to the brain bank of people who had had MS.

He lived 16 more years and died at age 96 in 2013.

Jonas Salk

Jonas Salk was described most often as nice, gentle and hardworking. Basil O'Connor said, "Jonas was the nicest, sincerest young man you ever met. There wasn't a mean or selfish bone in his body."

"He was one of the kindest, most considerate men I have ever known," said a nurse. "When you talked to him you felt that you were getting his undivided attention, even though you knew that he had his flu laboratory and his polio laboratory and his staff to think about. Whether you ran into him at six in the morning or at midnight you could count on a friendly greeting, the offer of a lift up or down the hill, the willingness to discuss a problem....He was just plain downright nice."

An administrator at the D.T. Watson Home for Crippled Children where Salk first tested his vaccine said, "He was charming and gentle—we have never seen him otherwise...a man deeply concerned about the human importance of the experiment."[42]

His first wife Donna said, "He perseveres and perseveres and things eventually work out by which time he begins to persevere at something else."[43]

Most scientists wanted to learn everything there is about polio. But Salk's motive was to find a vaccine and find it soon to stop children from dying or becoming paralyzed. John Enders and Albert Sabin believed it could take up to ten years to come up with a live vaccine.[44] Salk said he could come up with a killed vaccine in 12 to 15 months.[45]

People were clamoring for a vaccine. There was a large generation of babies born between 1946 and 1964 that they were worried about. They were tired of giving money to the March of Dimes and seeing nothing for their efforts. The NFIP needed a scientist with a sense of urgency. Salk, concerned about his own three children and all children was the man they chose to back.

Jonas Salk, born in 1914, was the son of Russian immigrants who had come to New York to escape the bloody pogroms. They encouraged all three of their sons to get an education. All three became doctors but Jonas was the most gifted. His mother predicted that he was the son who would become famous. At age twelve he entered Townsend Harris High School in New York City, a difficult school to get into but it allowed students to graduate in three years. It prepared him for City College which in the 1930s and 1940s produced more Nobel Prize winners and PhD recipients than any other public college except the University of California at Berkeley.

Jonas wanted to study law so that he could enter politics and do some good for the country. But at City College he discovered science and loved it. At the end of his freshman year he took a year's leave of absence to study biochemistry. Then he returned to his medical class. Eventually he became a laboratory worker under Dr. Thomas Francis, Jr.[46]

Thomas Francis was a first rate microbiologist. He discovered the Type B influenza virus at the Rockefeller Institute. He was of medium height with a mustache and a wry sense of humor. He liked Salk and found him "extremely able."[47]

Since Francis was engaged in research into influenza which had killed almost as many soldiers as were killed in battle in World War I, Salk wasn't drafted during World War II. He worked six years doing influenza research under Francis. The NFIP only gave him a grant of $2100 a year to find a vaccine for influenza. Since there are more than 100 strains of influenza, they had to put as many strains as possible into one vaccine.[48]

Francis and Salk's first experiment was a success. It produced a strong antibody response to the flu. But subsequent experiments were less effective. The vaccine only works if it contains the proper flu strain for the current season.[49]

Salk wanted more independence. He was offered his own lab in Pittsburgh. He went there in October of 1947 and resumed his influenza studies. He became the director of a virus research program.[50] He hoped to study polio, influenza, measles and the common cold in that order.[51]

During World War II, little research was done on polio. Modern laboratory machines, materials, lab assistants and scientists were needed for research. This would require a big grant from the NFIP. In the fall of 1947 Jonas Salk became an associate professor of bacteriology and microbiology at Pittsburgh.[52] By 1949 people were ready for some form of polio prevention or cure.

A vaccine grown in nervous tissue could cause a fatal inflammation of the brain. It was believed that polio could be grown in non-nervous tissue since it seemed to grow in the intestines. That would make a vaccine possible. Scientists preferred a drug to a vaccine but no drug ever cured a virus.[53]

The first step was to find out how many types of polio virus there were so that the vaccine would contain all types. It was known that there were at least three but what if there were more than three? Scientists also had to identify all the strains of virus in each type. The work would not be challenging. Graduate students and technicians could do it. Young, hungry scientists like Salk could do it. The work was described by one writer as "stupefyingly dull." Four laboratories worked on the typing. Salk completed the work first.[54]

Others helped him and they worked fifteen hour days. A lab worker said later, "We worked like dogs. It was like a factory, but those of us who knew how unusual that kind of speed-up was in a university lab did not mind, because we felt we were part of a closely knit team engaged in a great effort."

Salk was given an NFIP grant of $200,000 a year to do this work.[55]

Many monkeys were used for the typing project. The virus typing program cost $1,190,000 mostly because monkeys were so expensive to buy, maintain and dispose of.[56] Rhesus monkeys were sacred in India. They were believed to be incarnations of the monkey god Hanuman. The Indian authorities allowed them to be sold as long as only non-Hindus captured them and they weren't mistreated. They often became sick from dysentery, pneumonia, worms and other diseases. Many died on the way over.

They'd come over weak from their long trip. O'Connor created a sort of Warm Springs for monkeys in South Carolina where they could rest and recuperate before undergoing the trying lab tests.

Rhesus monkeys had been plentiful but were brought to the brink of extinction by American scientists. Indian authorities finally halted their exportation in 1978.[57] Other monkeys used were chimpanzees because they could catch and transmit polio. They were susceptible to nearly every other human disease. In 1966 wild African chimps experienced a polio epidemic. They caught polio from human beings living nearby.[58]

In 1949 Dr. John Enders, Dr. Thomas H. Waller and Dr. Frederick G. Robbins made a discovery which saved the lives of thousands of monkeys. It also made possible the creation of a vaccine that could inoculate millions of people. While growing chicken pox virus in a culture of non-nervous human tissue, they found they had a few test tubes left over. They decided to put some poliovirus in them. The virus grew.[59]

This was great news. Nervous tissue could cause allergic brain damage and there were not enough monkeys to provide the amount of vaccine that was needed. Now, 200 cultures could be prepared from one monkey's kidney. "It was like hearing a canon go off," said Tom Rivers. [60]

In 1954 Enders, Weller and Robbins received the Nobel Prize in medicine for their 1949 discovery of how to culture polio virus in non-nervous tissue.

Salk was the first person to ask for the culture. He wrote Harry Weaver, the research director of the NFIP, on September, 7, 1949, "You mentioned Dr. Ender's work on virus grown on foreskin tissue-culture. If you could arrange for us to get some of Dr. Ender's material, we would like very much to try to immunize a few monkeys with it."

He began to set up his lab to provide vaccine.

Salk had decided what strains to use in his vaccine. For Type I he would use the virulent Mahoney strain from an Ohio family. For Type II he would use the MEF-1 strain found in Egypt in 1942. Type III would be the Saukett strain named after a boy whose stool sample he had kept.

On June 16, 1950 he announced that he was ready to begin studies of polio prevention.[61]

In March of 1951 scientists met in Hershey, Pennsylvania and decided that the time for experimentation on humans had arrived.[62]

In September of 1951 Salk went to the Second International Poliomyelitis Congress at the University of Copenhagen. "During the voyage," he said, "it became obvious that I was a nice young whippersnapper from Pittsburgh going to Denmark to report on some drudgery I had performed."[63]

On the way back he met O'Connor's daughter Bettyann Culver who was partially paralyzed in 1950 with "some of Daddy's polio." She was thirty-years-old and had five children. Mrs. Culver was concerned. She thought she should have recovered by now. Salk comforted her. O'Connor said of him:

> He is aware of the world and concerned about it. He sees beyond the microscope. He takes an overview. He tries to see how things fit together, not just in the laboratory but in the whole shooting match. He's a generalizer and a synthesizer. For someone with a legal mind like mine this is impressive. I am less impressed by the sort of mind that gets bogged down in fringe details.

O'Connor was 61-years-old and a victim of a heart attack. He wanted to *lick* polio before he died. Salk was in a hurry too to bring out a vaccine to protect children from polio. Both O'Connor and Salk came from immigrant stock and understood each other. Both had "formidable minds" and were humanists. When they first met, O'Connor needled Salk and Salk surprised everyone by needling the great man back. They began to write and call each other often. [64]

Experiments were traditionally done on people who didn't understand what was being done to them such as children and retarded people. On February 27, 1950, Hilary Koprowski had fed a live polio vaccine to children.[65]

Tom Rivers felt uneasy about the testing, "An adult can do what he wants but the same does not hold true for a mentally defective child. Many of these children did not have mommas and papas, or if they did their mommas and papas didn't give a damn about them."[66]

All three vaccine pioneers: Koprowski, Salk and Sabin broke ethical guidelines established in 1947 because of Nazi experiments.

Salk decided to test the children at the D.T. Watson Home for Crippled Children. It wasn't much of a risk. Many of the children had already had polio.

He took before and after injection blood samples and found that his killed vaccine provoked a stronger antibody response than did the original virus. While he was waiting for results, he called and visited the children often to make sure they were okay. He knew the children by name and they loved to have him visit.

He also tested the Polk State School for retarded male children and adults. He tested their before and after antibody levels as well.[67]

He was thrilled when the Polk State School trials were successful. One test subject from the Watson Home wrote:

> *Dr. Salk is a happy Man*
> *I am proud of Him*
> *he discovered a safe vaccine to fight polio*
> *and I hope No one else Gets Polio*
> *and May God Bless Him*
> *From your Pal, Peter Herwatic*

The money rolled in. Between 1949 and 1953 he got almost a million in grants from the NFIP plus $255,000 for indirect costs. The army gave him $140,000 for his influenza research.

During the polio season of 1952 more children died from polio than from any other communicable disease. The polio season had been unusually long. It had gone from Memorial Day until well into October. It was the worst year ever.[68] Salk felt pressured to hurry. He extended his trials to 600 Pittsburgh children.[69]

The Committee on Immunization met in Hershey on January 24, 1953. Two days later Harry Weaver hinted that a big announcement was about to come out. Earl Wilson's gossip column said, "NEW POLIO VACCINE—BIG HOPES SEEN."[70]

Salk wanted to let the public know that a vaccine would not be available for the next polio season but as a scientist he was supposed to publish his work before presenting it to the public. He decided it was more important to be honest with the public. On March 26, 1953 he went on a radio program called *The Scientist Speaks for Himself.*

He spoke calmly and clearly, explaining the progress made so far on the polio front.

He explained that in 1909 polio was discovered to be a virus. A 1951 study showed that three types of the virus exist. A person who has had one type of the virus is not immune to the other two types. Antibodies from a vaccine would prevent polio from reaching the cells of the spinal cord and brain. A successful vaccine would cause antibodies in the blood which could fight all three virus types.[71]

In 1949 Dr. John Enders discovered that polio virus could be grown in test tubes containing living tissue. Now we are able to create the virus without storing it in monkeys. The material must be made harmless but effective (that is, contain antibodies against polio) in immunizing human beings. Monkeys were tested first.

When humans were tested the vaccine was found to be safe. It also increased the levels of antibodies.

There are still more experiments to be done and "many questions that remain to be answered." Experiments are still in progress, "many are quite incomplete." In the most recent study the amount of antibody induced "compares favorably with that which develops after natural infection."

There is "justification for optimism." "There will be no vaccine available for widespread use for the next polio season." We must "move cautiously...step by step."

The next day the vaccine was front page news. Most papers emphasized that the vaccine would not be ready for the next polio season.[72]

Stories about Salk and his vaccine appeared in *Life, Time, Collier's, Consumer Reports, Popular Mechanics, School Life, U.S. News and World Reports and Newsweek. Science News Letter* printed weekly updates on the vaccine.[73]

In 1953 Salk inoculated his wife Donna and their children Peter, nine, Darrell, six and Jonathan, three.

In May he inoculated local school children in Pittsburgh. He found by experimentation that he would need less Formalin at a temperature closer to the temperature of the human body.

On January 23 and 24th at the Hotel Hershey, Salk presented the results of his trials. The scientists there realized that his vaccine would have to be tested on a much larger group of people before it could be approved.[74]

Basil O'Connor took him aside and said:

Nobody is breathing down your neck. It's your work and nothing will be done with it that you don't want done. You have my word on it. But just tell me one thing: Do you think it is possible—all I mean is possible—that you might come up with something for field trial by the end of this year or the beginning of next?

"Yes," said Salk. "It's possible."

Salk said later, "We understood each other perfectly, as only a couple of crazy guys like us can."

O'Connor decided that before a trial could begin, the government should become involved. If all went well with the trial, the government could push the vaccine. If there were any problems they would be reported to the National Institutes of Health (NIH) which might take some of the heat off of the NFIP.

People in the NIH had trouble believing that the polio virus would be killed when exposed to Formalin. "We needed to be satisfied that Salk's recipe could be applied successfully by industry before we could rest easily with this thing." So they insisted that the antiseptic Merthiolate be added to each batch of the vaccine. Unfortunately the Merthiolate weakened the vaccine and some of the shots had to be given over again at Salk's insistence.[75]

By February 23, 1954 Salk had personally inoculated 5,000 children in his town of Pittsburgh. He stated that he had not established what the length of time should be between booster shots. He would spend much time on this problem and on trying to discover whether or not his vaccine would provide lifelong immunity.

The Field Trial

Albert Sabin was saying a field trial would be premature to which Salk replied that 7,000 people had already been safely injected and found to be immune to polio. [76]

During a meeting of scientists discussing field trial problems, O'Connor started jotting numbers down on a piece of paper. He was usually respectful of scientists but to their surprise he clearly and forcibly spoke up, "I have just figured out that during this coming summer 30 or 40,000 children will get polio. About 15,000 of them will be paralyzed and more than a thousand will die. If we have the capacity to prevent this, we have a social responsibility here that none of you have been talking about. Let me remind you that we are supported by the people and it is our duty to save lives, no matter how many difficulties may be involved."[77]

In 1953, Thomas Francis was asked to direct the field trial. He insisted that it be a double-blind field trial. Half of the substance given would be a harmless, inert placebo. Half would be the vaccine. No one would know who got what.[78]

Adults, it was thought, had already been exposed to polio at some point in their lives. The vaccine would have to be tested on children.[79]

In 33 states the second grade would get the vaccine. The first and third grades would get the placebo. In 11 states one half of the first, second and third grades would get the placebo and one half would get the vaccine.[80] Francis insisted that he be free of "external influence." He thought it very important to be independent of the NFIP.

The data about the children would be kept on IBM cards and it would contain 144 million items of information.[81]

The NFIP gave out grants to pay for the trial. A statistician was asked to predict areas and counties of 50,000 to 200,000 people that were likely to be hit hard during the next polio season. The statistician's predictions were remarkably accurate. Nearly 2 million children would be tested from those areas. Some would have blood tests to test their antibodies.

The test involved thousands of volunteers. The NFIP had 250,000 full time volunteers who were anxious to help. 20,000 doctors, 40,000 nurses, 14,000 principals, 50,000 teachers eagerly volunteered also.[82] Everyone was anxious to help.

The children, called *Polio Pioneers* were given illustrated picture books to explain what they would be going through and why. If asked, they would explain that no one would know who was getting the "real stuff" and who was getting the "harmless stuff." When asked by one adult why some would be getting medicine that wouldn't do them any good, the children were shocked by his ignorance. "Those youngsters gave as good a description of a double-blind study as I have ever heard," he said. [83]

It looked like there would not be enough syringes to go around but just in the nick of time a surgical supply company produced a new disposable syringe.

Parents were given forms to sign. At first the form was going to be entitled *Consent Form*. At the last minute someone suggested calling it a *Request Form*. Who wouldn't request that their child get a polio vaccine?[84]

The *Polio Pioneers* were enjoying the attention. They wondered if it would hurt. Would they get the "real stuff"? They enjoyed reading the illustrated story books. The books were about them after all.

On April 4, 1954, two weeks before the trial was to begin, syndicated gossip columnist Walter Winchell, no longer as popular as he once was, went on the radio and said, "Good evening, Mr. and Mrs. America, and all the ships at sea."

"In a few moments I will report on a new polio vaccine—it may be a killer!" He claimed that the NFIP had been storing hundreds of thousands of little white coffins for the children who would die during the field trial.

The "little white coffins" and the virulent Mahoney strain being used gave the Vaccine Advisory Committee pause. The committee consisted of a group of experts who were supposed to give the go-ahead for the trial. They discussed the numbers of children who would die or be paralyzed each year that the vaccine was put off. They were told that the safety tests had worked. They were reminded that 5,000 children in Pittsburgh had been vaccinated with no ill effects.

Finally they took a vote and recommended that the field trial begin. When the official resolution had been written they had removed a lot of legalese. Now, they put it back in. This trial was too important to recommend in layman's language.

Everyone wanted a copy of it. O'Connor said, "The only way to make it better would be to pin it to a thousand dollar bill."

The next morning the vaccinations began.[85]

Six-year-old Randy Kerr from McLean, Virginia was the first *Polio Pioneer* to get the shot. He said, "I could hardly feel it. It hurt less than a penicillin shot."[86]

Black children were vaccinated outside. They were not allowed in the white schools where the vaccinations were taking place. Their parents were relieved that they had gotten out the word that black children got polio too. They were not upset. They expected the discrimination. "This was the thing that was terrible," a nurse said. "They just thought this is how it had to be for them." [87]

Thomas Francis had set up his Vaccine Evaluation Center in an old maternity hospital in Ann Arbor, Michigan. Salk's first two sons had been born there. By the end of June the vaccinations were over. Thomas Francis was kept very busy tabulating the results of the trial. On July 12, his wife Dorothy was involved in a car crash and spent six months in the hospital. He somehow found the time to visit her three times a day.[88]

In the meantime, Salk perfected his vaccine. He found a faster way to produce it, looked into changing the inactivation period and the interval between booster shots.

Tests showed that some lots had deteriorated because of the Merthiolate.[89]

In 1954 the NFIP was out of money. The cost of the field trial, the gamma globulin shots which provided a little protection against polio (they were supposed to strengthen the immune system), and the aid to patients had depleted their resources. The NFIP had an emergency fund-raising campaign in August which helped buy vaccine for the Spring of 1955. But it still wasn't enough money. 9 million dollars had already been paid to Cutter Laboratories, Eli Lilly, Pitman-Moore, Wyeth Laboratories, Sharp & Dohme, and Parke, Davis. The vaccine would be given free-of-charge in 1955.[90] The NFIP had already spent 7 million on the field trial. Basil O'Connor who was in charge of NFIP finances wanted to know how the vaccine evaluation was going.

Thomas Francis couldn't tell him. He didn't know. When he did know, he would tell Salk first, then the world.

O'Connor was also worried because the pharmaceutical houses were saying they would produce a vaccine even if it was only 15 to 35% successful as long as it was safe. O'Connor said, "I am not at all sure that they will not bring one out that wasn't effective at all provided it is safe. Now these are the facts of life to face."

This middle ground was not good at all. It would mean they had not *licked* polio. But the public might be satisfied with these inadequate results and stop giving to the March of Dimes. They might think the war against polio had been won.[91]

In June of 1954 the field trial was complete. Merthiolate was eliminated from the vaccine. Thomas Francis predicted he would finish tabulating the results by February or March of 1955. Then he would analyze the figures and write his report. There would be no time to publish the findings for his peers so the American Journal of Public Health offered to publish a supplement in the May issue and Eli Lilly offered a closed-circuit telecast for 54,000 physicians. The announcement of the results would be April fifth or April twelfth. The report was not ready on April fifth. The announcement would be April twelfth. "Do you know the significance of that day?" O'Connor asked NFIP executives. No one did. "It will be the tenth anniversary of Roosevelt's death."

He said later, "Some day I hope to run across a coincidence that will not be blamed on me. I had no more to do with holding that meeting on Roosevelt's anniversary than you did. But nobody believes me."[92]

It was 13 years to the day that Jonas Salk had first arrived in Ann Arbor to do lab work, but no one noticed.[93]

The announcement would take place at Ann Arbor. Donna Salk said, "Jonas said that this was likely to be a special thing and we all should go....We arranged to go, expecting to return the day after the meeting." [94]

Salk said later, "I was totally unprepared for what happened at Ann Arbor."[95]

Some information had leaked to the press. "Hey, Bill," one reporter said. "You all set for the story." "What story?" he replied. "Jesus Christ, there ain't even any meat left on the bone."

People came from Pittsburgh expecting a positive report. There had been fewer polio cases in the nation in 1954 and that was encouraging.

Jonas and his family stayed at a private estate owned by the university. Jonas was told at breakfast that results were favorable. Other visitors got rooms on campus. The press got the release at 9:10. It began, "The vaccine works. It is safe, effective, and potent." Reporters grabbed the release and yelled into telephones, "IT WORKS! IT WORKS!," "VICTORY OVER POLIO," " POLIO VACCINE WORKS."

Tom Rivers described the scene, "God it was just a madhouse, it really was! I don't know when I've seen such wild people!" "Wholesale chaos." Scientists said, "The bedlam was revolting."

Inside the auditorium scientists sat quietly while short, chunky Dr. Francis dressed in a black suit, white shirt and striped gray tie read his report. It was called *An Evaluation of the 1954 Poliomyelitis Vaccine Trials – the summary report.* He said, "The field trials and evaluation were made possible by a grant from the NFIP totaling $7,500,000."

Francis spoke for one hour and thirty-eight minutes. The vaccine was 60-70% effective against Type I. It was over 90% effective against Type II and Type III. It was 94% effective against the frightening bulbar polio which inhibited breathing.

It had been proven to be safe.

Salk got up to talk about his recommendations for the frequency of booster shots. He also thanked "everybody on earth" except for the people from the Virus Research Lab, some of whom went home in tears, and Dr. Francis who had evaluated the vaccine. He said his new formula might reach 100% effectiveness. Francis said, "What the hell did you have to say that for? You're in no position to claim 100% effectiveness. What's the matter with you?"[96]

The release time for the full report was supposed to be 10:20 am but Dave Garroway, host of NBC's *Today* show, jumped the gun. "The vaccine works," he said. "it is safe, effective and potent." At 10 am the radio was played on loud speakers in schools, factories and stores. It gave most of the details. Bells rang, horns honked, people shouted, women cried, men hugged. "IT WORKS! IT WORKS!" People yelled.

"We were safe again," a *Polio Pioneer* said later. "At our desks we cheered as if the Orioles or the Colts had won a big game. Outside we could hear car horns honking and church bells chiming in celebration. We had conquered polio."[97]

The scientists were unaware of the celebration. They were saying, "Anyone could have done it." But *Salk* had done it and done it *first.*

That night, Edward R. Morrow had Salk on his half-hour television program *See It Now.* He was the only man who impressed Salk. Salk said later, "Ed Murrow was not trivial. I found myself responding at the level I like to respond to. I found him introspective, meditative, with a purity of thought. He had true pitch."

He told Murrow that the real victory over polio would come in the year when there would be little or no paralytic polio. He praised the people for giving to the March of Dimes. When Murrow asked, "Who owns the patent on this vaccine?" Salk said, "Well, the people I would say. There is no patent. Could you patent the sun?"[98]

Salk became a hero. Publicist Thomas J. Coleman said, "Jonas was slow to catch on to what was happening.... He was behaving as if the situation would blow over in a few hours." His wife was "appalled" by the hero worship and wanted to change her name to Smith.

When the Salks got home they found a ton of telegraphs, mail, offers for hundreds of awards, and a plan to erect a statue of Salk. Salk became edgy and his son Peter said, "Dad, I'd rather be an ordinary person like me than famous and bothered like you." Five-year-old Jonathan Salk got a phone call from a friend who had seen him on television. "Oh yes," he said. "I'm famous and so is my father."

Salk tried to find some privacy but it was impossible. He received an honorary degree, a medallion and a medal struck in his honor. An artist in Norway painted his picture.[99] Reporters and photographers followed him around, people donated money and gifts. Paul Winchell, the ventriloquist who had had polio as a child, asked his viewers to send money to Dr. Salk. The phone rang off the hook and they had to get an answering service and a new number for their own personal use.[100]

On April 22, 1955, Salk was asked to bring his wife and children to the White House to receive a citation from President Eisenhower. He was told to accept the award and simply say, "Thank you, Mr. President." But he insisted on giving a little speech. The president handed the award to Salk with tears in his eyes saying, "I have no words to thank you. I am very, very happy." Later he said, "I'm so glad my grandson has been inoculated. I'm just waiting till my granddaughters are old enough."[101]

Salk then said these words, "If I were to say that I'm honored on this occasion, I would not be telling the whole truth. I say, rather, that on behalf of all the people, in laboratories in the field, and those behind the lines, I gladly accept this recognition of what each of us has contributed, and I hope that we may have the opportunity to see again in our lifetime, the beginning of the end of other fears that plague mankind."

Then Eisenhower turned to the boys and said, "Let's go back in, boys." He gave a ballpoint pen and a pocket knife to each boy. Darrell Salk asked, "What else do you do besides play golf?" "I paint and fish," the President replied. This produced a long description of Darrell's latest painting he had done in school.

The government had taken part in the field trial. It was decided that any problems with the vaccine would be reported to the government so that problems wouldn't be blamed on the NFIP. No one in the government understood polio. Tom Rivers said, "The Public Health Service would eventually have to license the vaccine and nobody in the Public Health Service knew anything about polio. So we got them tangled up in this mess, and we had an awful time teaching them about polio."[102]

On April 11, 1953 the Federal Security Agency had been renamed the Department of Health, Education and Welfare. It included the Public Health Service which included the National Institutes of Health and the National Institute of Microbiology. The National Institute of Microbiology included the Laboratory of Biologics Control which would rule on whether the vaccine should be licensed for commercial manufacture.

Mrs. Oveta Culp Hobby, the Secretary of Health, Education, and Welfare signed the official documents allowing inoculations to be given to millions of children.

She said, "It's a great day. It's a wonderful day for the whole world. It's a history-making day."[103]

Cutter Pharmaceutical Company had produced a popular diphtheria-pertussis-tentanus vaccine (DPT) in 1947. But when they called asking how often a live vaccine should get into the mix, one man panicked. He visited the next day and found conditions filthy with no safety precautions in place. He reported his findings to Salk who did nothing.[104]

On April 24, a child came down with polio. It had started at the vaccination site and paralyzed her arm. Then it spread to her respiratory muscles and she died. There were sixty cases in Idaho and California. In every case it was caused by the dangerous Type I Mahoney strain. Salk was devastated. The Cutter Vaccine was withdrawn and the vaccination campaign put on hold. In all, there were 204 cases of paralysis and 10 deaths. 61 of the victims had been vaccinated—the rest were people they had come into contact with. Live vaccine also contaminated Wyeth, Eli Lilly and Parke, Davis batches. They settled out of court. In an emergency session at the NIH, John Enders said to Jonas Salk, "It is quack medicine to pretend that this is a killed vaccine when you know it has live virus in it. Every batch has live virus in it." Jonas Salk felt that everyone in the meeting blamed him personally. He recalled, "This was the first and only time in my life that I felt suicidal. There was no hope, no hope at all." He went back to Pittsburgh and waited for the whole thing to blow over.[105]

A third of Cutter's test vaccine had had live virus in it and had to be thrown away. Cutter had been under no legal obligation to report this to the NIH. Salk said, "A thorough investigation of the reported cases is being made...." He knew that the problem had to have come from Cutter and not from the vaccine itself. Tom Coleman said, "He'd been through it all. He'd tested it all. He'd explored every angle of it. And he knew. This is what held him together."[106]

Fear was keeping children from being vaccinated. Physicians who had already given vaccines to relatives were afraid also.[107]

Salk said, "I cannot escape a terrible feeling of identification with these people who are getting polio." O'Connor said, "Salk was heartbroken. The poor kid....Nothing was wrong with his vaccine...but they [the government] pulled the vaccine off the market anyhow, and wrecked the public's confidence." [108]

The New York Times said, "Millions of parents fear that if their children don't get the vaccine they may get polio, but if they do get the vaccine, it might give them polio."[109]

Some safety tests recommended by Salk had not been done. A team of experts decided that any batch that did not pass safety tests had to be reported to the NIH.

The Surgeon General asked Cutter to remove their vaccine from the market. On May 6, 1955 he discovered that other manufacturers had had problems so on May 7 he stopped all vaccinations to evaluate their testing procedures. On May 13 the Parke, Davis vaccine was inspected and cleared for use. Eli Lily was cleared for use two days later. The rest of the companies were inspected and on May 27 Surgeon General Dr. Leonard A Scheele said the vaccinations could resume.[110]

On May 23 Scheele appointed a committee to set up new standards for safety tests, to choose a longer inactivation process and to require replacing the Mahoney strain with something less dangerous. The committee later required more filtration to prevent clumping that may have protected live virus from the Formalin. Because of the months of storage at Cutter, sediment had formed which may have protected the virus. Cutter also had neglected to perform three tests on inactivation rate suggested by Salk. And a third of their batches didn't pass their own safety tests and were discarded.[111] Only 36% of those allowed vaccine chose to be vaccinated in 1955.

People in high positions in the government were asked to resign or retire. and a big reorganization took place. On July 13, 1955 Oveta Culp Hobby resigned as Secretary of Health, Education and Welfare. On July 27 her special assistant resigned. On July 31 the director of the NIH retired.

The Laboratory of Biologics became a division of the NIH. The Communicable Disease Center was renamed the Centers for Disease Control (CDC) and the Surgeon General had all states report cases of poliomyelitis to the CDC. Because of the Cutter incident the federal government would have a strong hand in regulating biomedical products in the future.[112]

Salk predicted post-polio syndrome in his paper about the importance of early immunization against viruses. Many "viruses invade the CNS" (Central Nervous System). Do those viruses "disappear from the CNS" or do they "remain latent?" He was worried about common viruses such as measles and mumps as well as polio. It was already known that chicken pox could be reactivated as well as herpes simplex. "It would be of interest to know whether or not poliovirus infections could cause...damage to brain-stem centers that might not result in clinically manifest symptoms until a later time, under circumstances of growth, aging, or other stresses....[113] [They do.]

The first children to get the vaccine would be the 2 million *Polio Pioneers* who had gotten the placebo or were not injected at all during the field trial. The 400,000 children who had already been vaccinated would get a booster shot. The remaining vaccine would be given to first and second graders. These vaccinations would be given for free. [114]

In 1955, I was five-years-old and noticed a long line of "big kids" in the hallway. "What are they doing?" I asked someone. "They are getting shots." I knew what a shot was. I was glad I didn't have to get a shot. My husband, Greg, who was in second grade, was taken by his parents to a school auditorium where he and other kids got shots. His parents told him very firmly that this was a good thing and he would have to get one.

Joan H. remembered getting in line to get the vaccine. Another child who noticed she limped said, "Why are *you* getting this?" She was stunned by the question until she remembered that she had had polio and didn't need the vaccine.[115]

• • •

Salk continued to work on his vaccine. He wrote new inspection policies. He tested the length of time the immunity to polio lasted and when booster shots should be given. He attended many banquets which he felt were a waste of time.[116]

By 1962 there were only 910 cases of paralytic polio in the United States.[117]

With the help of money from O'Connor he designed and built a haven for artists, other humanists and philosopher-scientists on the ocean in San Diego. His people spent time on trying to unlock the secrets of cancer, muscular dystrophy, genetics, neurology and the immune system.[118] His wife divorced him in 1968 and a year later he met Francoise Gilot, a painter and the former mistress of Picasso.[119] He and his new wife spent much time away from San Diego. The humanists and scientist drifted away from his institute and Salk spent his time there alone watching hang-gliders, staring at the ocean, and writing books on philosophy.

• • •

The Salk vaccine had some imperfections. Scientists thought that one shot did not give lifelong protection. It didn't infect the gut which would have helped spread immunity. The syringes and needles were expensive making it difficult for poor people to afford the vaccination. The developing world could not afford it either and many people were afraid of needles.

Albert Sabin

ALBERT SABIN, M.D.

White-haired, dark-eyed, with a sharp nose, small, dark mustache, nubbin chin, and general mien of Reynard the Fox, Sabin is a sociable man and something of a gourmet; he also has a reputation in virological circles for asking the sharpest questions, in unctuous, Oxonian tones.—Greer Williams, *Virus Hunters*

Hilary Koprowski had tested his live vaccine on people even before Salk tested his killed one. And Koprowski tested it successfully in Poland, his homeland. Albert Sabin and Hilary Koprowski were too competitive to join forces. Albert Sabin got ready to start trials on people.[120]

Albert Sabin was arrogant, egotistical, cruel and a bully.[121] People described him as "a mean bastard," someone whose obituary everyone would like to read. [122] Someone said, "This was one mean guy...a nasty s.o.b." Hilary Koprowski would only say Sabin was a very good scientist. When Sabin died he wrote an obituary described as "glowing." Someone asked, "How could he stand to do that?" Another person said, "Easy. It meant Sabin was *gone*." [123]

Sabin was born Abram Sapersztein in 1906 in Bilystok in the Russian Empire. He and his family moved to the United States to escape the pogroms.

An uncle paid his college tuition on the condition that he would become a dentist. In 1923 he went to pre-dental school but found that he hated dentistry. His interest turned to medical research and his uncle cut off all support.

He took William Hallock Park's course in bacteriology. Park got Sabin a scholarship to New York University and a job.[124]

He joined the Rockefeller Institute in 1935 and worked under Peter Olitsky, the expert in neurotropic viruses. Sabin wrote a paper that predicted that polio virus would be grown in tissue culture. He studied and concluded that the virus did not enter through the nose as Flexner had said, a theory that had wasted years. He dug into the role of the intestines in nursing the virus. In 1940 he got a grant of $7,000 from the NFIP. During the war he tried, but failed, to develop a vaccine against insect-bourne viral encephalitis.[125]

In 1946 he mentioned that an oral vaccine could be created to provide life long immunity against polio. As Salk worked on his killed vaccine, Sabin said dead vaccines were useless and dangerous especially since Salk might not be able to inactivate the deadly type I Mahoney strain he was using.

He developed a live, oral vaccine and proposed testing it on children from Willowbrook School on Staten Island with Downs syndrome and other severe learning disabilities. The NFIP would not allow this so in 1954 and 1955 he inoculated prisoners in the Federal Reformatory at Chillicothe, Ohio. All thirty prisoners developed antibodies to the three virus types and no one got polio.[126]

One dose protected a person for life. It took only days to work, not weeks. The weakened virus would be shed in the vaccinated person's feces providing immunity to unvaccinated people.[127]

Sabin needed to test a much larger group of people. Too many people in this and other countries were already immune to polio because of the Salk vaccine.

Russia had a big problem with polio which had never been addressed.[128]

A group of Russians asked permission to visit Sabin. This was just what he had been hoping for. While they were there, he asked if he could go back to visit his homeland. He was invited a month later and went to the Soviet Union to lobby for his vaccine. When he got home, he sent them a virus sample for testing.[129]

In 1959 the Russians vaccinated ten million children. Then, the Russian Health Ministry ordered vaccinations for every person under the age of twenty. The World Health Organization (WHO) sent a scientist to Russia to verify the results and found the Sabin vaccine safe and effective. They also found a marked reductions of cases in 1959.[130]

By 1962 polio was almost extinct in the United States because of the Salk vaccine. Polio was now rare—just a "medical curiosity." But the Public Health Service insisted that even people who had been inoculated against polio had to take the Sabin vaccine at a cost to the people of $75 million. The Sabin vaccine was considered better than the Salk. The Russians had the best vaccine and this was unacceptable. They were already winning the space race and were better at the sciences. Why should Russia have a better vaccine?

In 1961 the American Medical Association (AMA) recommended that the Salk vaccine be replaced when the Sabin vaccine became available.[131] On August 17, 1961 the Public Health Service licensed Sabin Type I. On October 10, 1961 Type II was licensed. On March 27, 1962 Type III was licensed.[132]

In 1963 people unprotected by the Salk vaccine were catching polio from friends and relatives who got the Sabin vaccine. In June of 1964 the Public Health Service discovered that at least 57 cases of paralytic polio were caused by the oral vaccine. As many adults as children were getting the disease. Polio did more damage to adults than to children so adults were quietly advised not to get the vaccine. Few people listened. The Sabin vaccine was highly advertised. The warning was not. One writer considered using the Sabin vaccine rather than the Salk vaccine "an exercise in madness."[133]

People who took care of vaccinated infants could get polio. People with compromised immune systems were also at risk. Children also got it. The AMA reassured physicians that people who had already gotten the Salk vaccine would not be harmed by the oral vaccine.[134]

Salk was angry. He said, "We have reached the point where the dominant cause of polio in this country is the [live] vaccine itself." He said this was not acceptable particularly when "a killed vaccine exists that cannot possibly cause polio." Salk encouraged people who had gotten polio to contact an attorney. In December of 1974 a couple was awarded $200,000 from a manufacturer of the vaccine that had given their child polio. At this point drug manufacturers and doctors began to realize they would have to warn consumers of the danger.[135]

In 1964 the National Institutes of Health predicted that if problems continued with the oral vaccine, it would be withdrawn from the market. A Russian doctor said, "For swift immunization requiring the fewest possible separate doses, purified killed vaccines are the thing." [136]

As a safety measure in 1996 the United States started to vaccinate children first with the Salk vaccine and later with the Sabin vaccine. That didn't help. The United States continued to average twelve paralytic polio cases a year until 2000 when they switched back to the Salk vaccine alone. The Sabin vaccine is used for developing nations because of its ease of use. Once polio is eliminated from those countries there will probably be a continuing effort to use the Salk vaccine.[137]

Albert Sabin's wife, Sylvia, killed herself in 1966 on Sabin's 60th birthday. He moved to Israel in 1969.

While living in Israel, he met Heloisa, a Brazilian woman. He had his first heart attack a few months before meeting her and his second a month after meeting her. He was asking if he could leave the hospital when he had his third heart attack. He left Israel for the Cleveland Clinic and was told he would have to have open heart surgery. After a long recovery, he flew to Palm Beach to rest. He then returned to Israel with Heloisa and got married. He left laboratory research in 1974 for a research professorship at the Medical University of South Carolina. By that time people had noticed that his oral vaccine was giving them polio.

He died in 1993 at the age of 87.

His tombstone says:

> SABIN
> Developer of the vaccine that made possible
> the global eradication of poliomyelitis.[138]

Warm Springs honored seventeen polio heroes—Roosevelt; O'Connor; three 19th century physicians; twelve 20th century scientists.[139]

Thomas Francis died in 1969.

Basil O'Connors wife died suddenly in 1955. In 1957 he married Hazel Royale, a physical therapist at Warm Springs. His daughter Bettyann Culver died in 1961. His younger daughter, Sheelagh, died in 1966. Basil

O'Connor, now called "a man without a disease," died in 1972 at age 80 while conducting Foundation business. He had *licked* polio in his lifetime.[140] He was praised for creating a "unique social invention: a permanently self-sustaining source of funds for the support of research—the voluntary health organization."[141]

Global Polio Eradication Initiative

By 1980 polio was eradicated in the United States. In 1994 it was extinct in the Americas. By the year 2000 it was gone from the Western Pacific. By 2002 it was eradicated in Europe. By 2012 it was gone from India.

The Global Polio Eradication Initiative (GPEI) was formed in 1988. Its goal was to eradicate polio by the year 2000. In 1988 350,000 people were paralyzed a year. By January 2011 there were only 222 cases of polio. Pakistan, Afghanistan and northern Nigeria were the only countries not vaccinated. If these countries are not vaccinated, an epidemic could start and trigger as many as 200,000 cases of polio.[142]

In these countries people who allow their children to be vaccinated are subject to beatings. The tropical heat and difficult terrain makes vaccination difficult. Mistrust of Westerners has caused fierce resistance to vaccination.

Dr. Datti Ahmed said:

> *Polio vaccines are corrupted and tainted by evildoers from America and their Western allies... We believe that modern-day Hitlers have deliberately adulterated the oral polio vaccines with anti-fertility drugs and viruses which are known to cause HIV and AIDS.*[143]

In December of 2012, seven vaccinators had been shot dead in Pakistan.[144] Death threats and further murders have taken place and the vaccination program is now stalled. It is hoped that the people responsible for this realize that it is the disease that is evil, not the vaccinators.

6. Post-Polio Syndrome (PPS)

My battle with polio is not yet over.

—Peg Kehret

Camille Savard said:

> *I take note of how terrible it is to have suffered so much, with so much effort and work, only to find myself, today, back at the departure point.*[1]

Kathy H. said:

> *I thought it was in my past, I didn't realize it would so profoundly affect me later on in my life. Because so few survivors are left, they aren't doing any research on PPS. In another twenty years, we will all be gone.*[2]

Before my father was sixty, he began to tire easily. He said he was too tired to climb the steps to my parents' bedroom. He bought a bed and a little desk for the den on the first floor and slept there. He stopped going out for most family gatherings saying he was too tired. He retired in 1971 at age 62, he told me later, because he "felt awful." In 1977 he asked to be admitted to the hospital for tests to find out what was wrong with him. While there, he had a stroke and fell out of bed. When he came home he had to use a wheelchair. In 1979 he had another stroke and was put into a nursing home. He died of a third stroke in 1982 at age 72.

While recovering from polio most victims pushed themselves too much. Fatigue warns people to rest their muscles during exercise. Muscles affected by polio don't feel fatigue. When they first got polio survivors were advised to exercise. Post-polio syndrome is milder in people who ignored that advice.

One woman told to exercise says she was "either too foresighted or too slothful to engage in the strenuous exertion that would have put me back on my feet." Now victims of polio are being told to take it easy.[3]

In 1982 Dr. Lauro Halstead who got polio as a college student found himself getting overly tired. He would fall asleep at traffic lights and while driving a relatively short distance would have to pull off the road several times to rest. "I just felt this *extraordinary* sense of fatigue," he said. His legs became weak and it became more difficult to walk. He started driving to buildings he used to walk to and started taking the elevator rather than the steps. He lobbied for the Disabilities Act of 1990 which prohibits discrimination against the disabled and requires physical access to most public places.

By questioning the best in neurology, pathology, virus research and other fields and by ignoring polio experts he discovered that it takes 30 to 40 years for post-polio syndrome (PPS) to appear and that people in polio rehab had enlarged their muscle fibers to a huge extent practicing activities most of us take for granted. When they reach the age when any weight lifter's performance falls off, the victims of polio can no longer do some things they had considered easy.[4] Dr. Halstead now uses a motorized scooter.[5]. Before he got PPS he could walk.

In 1985 Richard L. Bruno, H.D., PhD appeared on *Nightline* with Albert Sabin to discuss the new problems facing polio survivors. In 1987 polio survivors were allowed to receive social security disability. Today there are at least 400,000 polio survivors in the United States.[6] 50% of polio survivors will get PPS. Even people with non-paralytic polio will get it.

The neurons that were not affected by polio are never the same. They became smaller and have shrunken axons.[7] These surviving motor neurons sent out new sprouts to activate the muscle fibers orphaned by polio. Perhaps the motor neurons can no longer activate the sprouts and they die.[8]

Fatigue is the most common symptom. Another common symptom is word-finding difficulty.[9]

Problems they are having include:

- insomnia
- trouble swallowing
- leg weakness
- low back pain
- joint pain
- sensitivity to cold
- sensitivity to anesthesia
- difficulty breathing
- weakness in the limb that had not been paralyzed

One doctor described PPS as becoming weaker and tireder.[10]

The survivors of polio have been overworking their surviving motor neurons all their life. After age 60, when motor neurons begin to deteriorate in healthy people, the polio survivors begin to feel much worse—weaker with debilitating fatigue.[11]

William O. Douglass, a polio survivor and Supreme Court Justice exercised hard to become able bodied but later got what sounded like PPS.[12]

One person sought help only when the weakness turned to pain. It was difficult for her to stand for more than a few minutes and almost impossible to vacuum or make the bed.

Nancy C.'s fatigue and weakness caused her to give up her job.

Hugh Gallagher had to switch from a manual to electric wheel chair. In his 50s Leonard Kriegel switched from crutches to a wheelchair.[13]

Sharon K., who had polio in 1949, fully recovered but now has arthritis in the leg that was affected by polio. This affects her walking.[14]

Sarah C., who had no visible after effects of polio, has "rubbery" legs, is easily fatigued, has a brace on her left leg, went on disability, has an electric scooter, a van with a lift, and uses a walker or cane around the house.[15]

June A., who recovered from polio, now has numbness, pain, problems swallowing, weak legs and tires easily. [16]

Vivian H. who got polio in 1946 at age three-and-a-half could jump rope, roller skate and climb trees. She began to lose control of her diaphragm and now uses a C-PAP machine to help her breathe when she is sleeping.[17]

Clara R. who had never been paralyzed got PPS at age 60. She had to chew food well and take antibiotics for colds because they could turn into pneumonia. At age 70 she had to drink nutritional drinks and eat soft foods. In 2011 she had a feeding tube put into her stomach. She now breathes through a trach. She uses a nebulizer four times a day to keep her lungs clear. She is now 82.[18]

One man could get on the ground to do the weeding but when he got PPS, he could no longer get up. One woman described her fatigue as "insurmountable." One person could no longer negotiate four steps.[19]

One woman who had polio in 1953 said, "I could walk by myself when this [PPS] started. Then I needed a cane, then the walker, and now I'm using a power wheelchair....I told all of them I had polio and no one listened."[20]

One woman used to be able to walk, bike, hike and dance. With PPS she has to rest, use a cane, wheelchair and power scooter.[21]

Joan S. has weak legs, less endurance and can no longer ride a bike. "In these last ten years," she said, "I can't get up from a chair without exclusively using my arms."[22]

June F. uses a cane indoors now and a scooter for out-doors. She always uses the scooter in stores.[23]

Janice N. has begun to use oxygen and has been in and out of the hospital for respiratory failure. She has pain in her strong leg which has been doing all the work for her weak leg.[24]

Larry K.'s breathing became compromised and he now wears a brace on his arm.[25]

Katalin P. is "unable to move my foot to the pedals" and had to give up driving. When she moved to Denver, she experienced difficulty breathing and used oxygen at night.[26]

Lois F. went from walking sticks to a scooter.[27]

Leonard Kriegel fell thirty-nine years after having polio and discovered he could not get up.[28] In his 50s he discovered that he could no longer use long-legged braces and crutches because his elbows and shoulders could no longer handle it. "I would be a wheelchair tourist now," he said.[29]

He went to Paris and found it almost impossible to get around in a wheelchair. In France the people believed in the right to a pension, the right to an adequate diet and the right to public health care. Women's rights and the rights of the disabled had not occurred to them yet. The right of a wheelchair-bound person to cross the street and enter a museum also had not occurred to them.

He went up a sloping curb for the disabled person and found himself faced with a steep step. Men were working at the time making more wheelchair cuts. But when they were finished, "in front of each curb cut, making it impossible for me to mount the sidewalk, stood a small car."

He had to switch to his crutches and discovered that handicapped rest rooms had "wet and slippery" floors. In restaurants he either had to climb or descend steps to get to the rest room.[30]

On the other hand, while visiting San Francisco he noticed that the city was very wheelchair accessible. He said it was "a city in which wheelchair cuts in the curbs are as natural as flowers in the park."[31]

Jeane Dille began to have severe and constant back and shoulder pain because the nerves in the back of her neck were being compressed. She had an operation which helped but still had to quit her full time job and find a part time job where she could set the hours. She began to experience breathing problems and then fatigue. She even fell asleep in the hairdresser's chair. A BiPap ventilator worn at night helped her breathe better and lessened her fatigue and pain. When her right hand became weak she learned to use her left hand instead. Because of PPS she had to find hobbies she could do sitting down. She also started a post-polio group in her area.[32]

In her mid-forties Anne Finger was told, "Your nerves are not under your voluntary control. You cannot will them back."[33]

When PPS began to appear, Anne Finger went to a conference for people who had had polio:

> *I felt like an adoptee meeting her birth family for the first time at an enormous family reunion. Here I was surrounded by people who shared my personality quirks—my tough sense of humor, my drive, my big smile, my anger.*[34]

7. Dad

*Such people seem to be fulfilling themselves
and to be doing the best that they are capable
of doing....*

Abraham H. Maslow

Arnold Beisser had mystical experiences. He wrote:

*I had moments when I would experience that
limitless present—what the ancient wisdom had
called the "holy instant," when there was no
time and there were no divisions, and when I
was fully manifest.*[1]

Beisser became a great writer and psychiatrist. Did
my father have mystical experiences? I don't think so.

Arnold Beisser was ten years younger than Dad when he got polio and was stuck in an iron lung. Minutes seemed like hours and hours seemed like days. Arnold was desperate. Dad was a different story—mature, married, a father with a good job. Unlike Beisser he still had strong arms. Dad was proud of having beaten polio. He was proud of how skillfully he handled his crutches. He acted as if he was a celebrity or a war hero. His medals were his braces and his crutches.

He was weirdly calm. He accepted everything except what he saw as a direct assault on himself or his family. He accepted his disability and was proud of having survived the virus. He accepted us and all the neighborhood children even though we could be loud and obnoxious at times. Except for snow and ice which put a crutch walker in danger, he accepted the weather. It was never "too cold" or "too hot." He had a little smile on his face almost all the time.

I think Dad gradually came to be the man he was. By the time he got polio he was thirty-five, proud of himself and his family. And after polio he had a purpose which was to work for the organization that was paying for patient care and research into the prevention of polio.

Dad was a kind and good man because of the way he had lived and grown up. He was influenced by *all* his life experiences. I think polio made him more accepting of life's little annoyances. He never complained about pain although his arms sometime hurt from using crutches. He never complained that his braces were too heavy although they were. He never complained about being tired, yet he often was. He seemed happy and it seems to me that he had reached that state himself without a mystical experience.

He was born on November 22, 1909 in Federal Hill, Baltimore, Maryland. There is no record of his birth except in the family bible because in 1909 children born at home were not required to have a birth certificate. He was born in a row house a couple blocks north of General Butler's headquarters during the Civil War.

His father, Howard, was considered by a friend as "honest, trustworthy and capable." Dad picked up these same qualities. His mother, Lily, was a pretty English woman who had moved to Baltimore when her mother died. The couple moved from Baltimore to Norwalk, Ohio where their first child, a son Stanley, was born in 1898. When they left to come back to Baltimore the local paper said Howard had made "many warm friends" and helped out where ever he could including Bible class, the Brotherhood, teaching Sunday school and "aiding in the Boy Scout movement." Their only daughter Lillian was born in Baltimore in 1903. Dad was not Howard's favorite child and he sensed it. Lillian was beautiful and Stanley was a big, handsome boy.

None of the children were allowed to whine and complain which may explain Dad's complete lack of self pity. Howard never gave Dad any money. He told Dad to earn the money himself. He preached the value of hard work. Howard also said such things as work hard; go to church; get your proper rest; be ready for the next day *don't let the next day be ready for you*. Dad had probably heard this advice much too often. He did appreciate his father's financial advice: invest wisely; don't borrow; don't go into your principle; pay cash for everything. Howard was probably verbally abusive to Lily. Dad always said he was too strict with him. Lily had some mental health problems, mostly anxiety. She had a lot to do, clean house, cook, do the laundry. She worried over Dad's severe childhood asthma. Dad told me that she was the best woman he ever knew. She was kind, loving and quiet.

Dad had Attention Deficit Disorder (ADD) a neurological condition that makes it hard to pay attention and complete tasks. Usually the person with this disorder learns to somehow improve their concentration and stay on task. One symptom is being a risk taker. He learned to fly and buzzed people's houses. He once hit a tree but didn't notice it til after he landed and found a branch in his undercarriage. At age twenty he drove his Model A Ford on a round trip of 6000 miles to California. He loved to ride the roller coaster, drive his speed boat, dance, travel, ice skate, play badminton, fix cars and bowl.

Although Howard's business was losing money during the depression he helped other relatives out. Howard owned a wholesale canned food business. Dad didn't want to go to work for him but since he couldn't find any other job, he did. He did well as a salesman selling wholesale canned goods` to grocery stores. He was friendly and inquisitive. He got people to talk about themselves. My sister Anne said, "I was so proud of Dad. Everyone admired him and was his friend." He liked to ask everyone about their job. He asked his dentist whether he liked his job. "Yes," the dentist said, "but it is a lot of detail work." He asked why a young undertaker took up that work. "As a boy," he said, "I crossed through a graveyard to get to school. I always wondered what the bodies beneath me looked like." My father asked, "Did you find out?" He did. Once he had to help move their coffins to another cemetery. He opened the coffins to see what was in there. Most of the time there was only a little bit of dust. (They had been buried thirty or forty years.) But in perhaps 10% of the cases the long dead people looked like they had been buried yesterday. My father asked how this could happen. "No one knows," responded the young man.

He got married on November 21, 1933 the day before his twenty-fourth birthday in a simple ceremony in the church sanctuary.

He avoided being drafted during World War II by convincing a doctor to say his asthma was severe enough to keep him from fighting.

At work, his salary was high for the 1940s and he managed to save a lot of money. "You couldn't buy anything during the war," he explained.

Dad got polio in September of 1944. In Baltimore it is hot during early September and the polio season was not yet over. Baltimore was probably the polio capital of the world and he had chosen to stay and work near slums where polio was common. He counseled younger patients and made them laugh.

I was born in 1949—the year that John Enders and his associates had proven polio could be grown in non-nervous tissue culture. My brother Bud was born in 1951—the year the typing project was completed. My brother Bill was born in 1954—the year of the vaccine trial. Dad had been born in 1909—the year polio was discovered to be a virus.

Dad had compassion for others because he had been through polio. We had compassion for others because we felt sorry for Dad. Mom, who had always been pampered, grew angrier as the years went on. Now she had to take charge of things and wait on him. She made the important decisions and he let her.

On weekends he spent a lot of time out of doors sitting on the ground pulling weeds or pumping up the tires on the cars. We and other kids enjoyed following him when he was mowing the grass on the riding lawnmower. But on weekday evenings he only napped in front of the television.

In 1956 Bud and I got our first polio shot. Whenever we had to go back for a booster shot I would stand in the doctor's office and cry. Bud would run down the hall and try to get away. Afterwards Mom would take us to get a milkshake or some other fountain drink. In 1962 we were given a pink sugar cube—the oral vaccine. In rare cases that vaccine could cause polio. For example it caused the disease in my co-worker's husband and he was left with a bad limp.

While taking medicine to lower his blood pressure Dad became depressed. Friends told him to eat fresh oranges. When this didn't help, he probably discontinued the medicine.

By the time he was in his sixties, he was tired all the time and said he felt "awful." Because of the normal aging process and the overuse of their good muscles at least half of the people who had had polio came down with post-polio syndrome. He may have started getting this syndrome in his fifties.

In the 1970s Dad was watching television when something happened to his vision. The picture on the television set decreased to the size of a pinpoint. He called the eye doctor who came right over. The doctor realized it was a minor stroke. The doctor said, "What were you doing when this happened?" Dad said, "Watching television." The doctor said, "Television is a killer." He then asked who changes the channel. Dad said, "The kids do." The doctor said that he should at least get up and change the channel himself. From then on, he refused to let us change the channel.

It was too little too late. In 1977 Dad went to the hospital for tests, had a stroke and fell out of bed. He went into a coma for about a week. After he got out of the coma, everything had changed. First he had hallucinations, then was given a tricyclic antidepressant which made him manic. Mom stopped giving him the antidepressant and he went into a deep depression. He had two more strokes and died on August 24, 1982. Mom died on March 17, 2004.

Self Actualization

In spite of never having had a mystical experience Dad seemed to have most of the symptoms of self-actualization as described in Abraham Maslow's book *Motivation and Personality,* Chapter 11.

They are:

- absence of neurosis
- full use of talents
- needs for acceptance, love, self respect, knowledge and safety already fulfilled
- able to recognize dishonesty in others
- able to see reality correctly
- superior ability to reason and be logical
- inability to be threatened by the unknown
- find doubt and uncertainty to be a challenge
- acceptance of self and others
- lack of guilt and anxiety
- enjoy food, sleep and sex without inhibition
- distaste for hypocrisy

• • •

The one thing they do feel guilty about are their flaws that can be improved such as "laziness, thoughtlessness, loss of temper, hurting others."[2]

They are spontaneous, simple and natural. But will act conventional so as not to upset others. They do not like getting awards but will accept them "with the best possible grace."[3]

They like to focus on problems outside themselves. They don't see themselves as a problem. The problem they are working on may not be something they enjoy. They may see it as their duty to solve it.[4] They may try to solve a problem for the good of mankind, the good of a nation or the good of a few people in their family.

They have a "broader horizon" than others. This attitude imparts "a certain serenity and lack of worry…."

They can be alone "without discomfort." Almost all of them "like solitude."[5]

They are able to concentrate intensely which makes them seem absent-minded and detached from what is going on around them. People sometimes think they are snobbish or cold. The self-actualized person does not get as upset by their own troubles as do "normal people."

The self-actualized person is apt to have had sometime in their lives one or more mystical experiences. Maslow says mystical experiences are natural. He call them "peak experiences."

Self-actualized people are never unsure about the difference between right and wrong.[6]

Their sense of humor is not hostile. It is not superior. It does not rebel against authority. It is not smutty. It "pokes fun at human beings in general...who try to be big when they are actually small."[7] They poke fun at themselves but not in a masochistic way.

All of them are creative in their own way, if only in the way they perform an ordinary job. Their creativity is "more spontaneous, more natural, more human" than other people's.[8]

Most of them have a mission "to improve the world."

If Dad was not self-actualized I like to think that he was almost there. My guess is that Arnold Beisser, Jonas Salk, perhaps Jeane Dille and perhaps Louis Sternburg and maybe others mentioned in this book were.

End Notes

1. You Have Polio

[1.] Leonard Kriegel, *The Long Walk Home,* New York: Appleton-century Affiliate of Meredith Press Van Rees Press, 1964, 22 hereafter Long Walk

[2.] Gareth Williams, *Paralysed with Fear, The Story of Polio,* Palgrave: MacMillan, 2013, 92-93

[3.] Connie Anderson, editor, *How Ordinary People Overcame Extraordinary Challenges,* Minneapolis, MN: CAB Press, 2013, 193-194, hereafter Anderson

[4.] ibid, 19

[5.] ibid, 61

[6.] ibid, 263-264

[7.] Peg Kehret, *Small Steps: The Year I Got Polio,* Morton Grove, Illinois: Albert Whitman & Company, 1996, 11-13, hereafter Kehret

[8.] Tony Gould, A Summer Plague, Polio and its Survivors, New Haven & London: 1995, 297-299, hereafter Gould

[9.] Jeane L. Curey Dille, *Polio: A Dose of the Refiner's Fire, Surviving Polio,* Bloomington, Indiana: authorHOUSE, 2005, 13, hereafter Dille

[10.] ibid, 5

[11.] ibid, 5-12

[12.] ibid, 13

[13.] ibid, 12-16

14. Kriegel, 5-12
15. Leonard Kriegel, *Flying Solo, Reimagining Manhood, Courage, and Loss,* Boston: Beacon Press, 1998, 120, hereafter Kriegel
16. Charles L. Mee, *A Nearly Normal Life, a memoir,* Boston, Little, Brown and Company, 1999, 27-28, hereafter Mee
17. ibid, 17-20
18. Naomi Rogers, *Polio Wars, Sister Elizabeth Kenny and the Golden Age of American Medicine,* New York: Oxford University Press, 2014, 162
19. Gould, 288
20. Anderson, 25
21. ibid, 15
22. Williams, 28-29
23. Daniel J. Wilson, *Living with Polio, The Epidemic and Its Survivors,* Chicago: The University of Chicago Press, 2005, 45, hereafter Wilson
24. Kehret, 60
25. Richard L. Bruno, H.D., PhD, *The Polio Paradox, Uncovering the Hidden History of Polio to Understand and Treat "Post-Polio Syndrome" and Chronic Fatigue,* New York: Warner Books, Inc. 2002, 76, hereafter Bruno
26. Wilson, 119
27. ibid, 48-49
28. Gould, 236
29. Bruno, 76-77
30. Wilson, 121-122
31. Williams, 109-110
32. Black, 23
33. ibid, 23
34. David M. Oshinsky, *Polio, An American Story,* New York: Oxford University Press: 2005, 91
35. ibid, 29-31
36. Gould, 119

37. Bruno, 39-43
38. Gould, 224
39. ibid, 9
40. Anne Finger, *Elegy For A Disease, a Personal and Cultural History of Polio,* New York: St.Martin's Press, 2006, 46
41. Black, 43
42. Williams, 99-101
43. ibid, 94-95
44. ibid, 117-118
45. Black, 159
46. Gould, 7
47. *Guenter B. Risse, Revolt Against Quarantine: Community Responses to the 1916 Polio Epidemic, Oyster Bay, New York – Transactions & Studies of the College of Physicians of Philadelphia,* Ser. 5, Vol. 114, No. 1 (1992); 23-50 copyright 1992 by the College of Physicians of Philadelphia, 24-25
48. ibid, 25-26
49. ibid, 27-28
50. ibid, 29
51. ibid, 30-33
52. ibid, 34-35
53. ibid, 36-38
54. ibid, 41-45
55. ibid, 47
56. Mee, 5
57. Marc Shell, *Polio and its Aftermath, The Paralysis of Culture,* Cambridge, Mass: President and Fellows of Harvard College, 2005, 34, hereafter Shell
58. Louis and Dorothy Sternburg with Monica Dickens, *View from the Seesaw,* New York: Dodd, Mead & Company, 1986, 10-11, hereafter Sternburg
59. Bruno, 83
60. Anderson, 21
61. ibid, 41

[62.] Wilson, 33
[63.] Anderson, 183-184
[64.] Williams, 3
[65.] Mee, 4
[66.] Williams, 2
[67.] ibid, 112
[68.] Bruno, 56-57
[69.] Williams, 89-91
[70.] Oshinsky, 8-9

2. Rehabilitation

[1.] Rogers, 43
[2.] ibid, 44
[3.] ibid, 402
[4.] ibid, 418
[5.] Wilson, 99
[6.] ibid, 101
[7.] Sternburg, 37
[8.] Mee, 6
[9.] Arnold Beisser, *Flying Without Wings, Personal Reflections on Loss, Disability, and Healing,* New York, Toronto, London, Sydney, Auckland: 1990, 105, hereafter Beisser
[10.] ibid, 105-107
[11.] Kehret, 57
[12.] Dille, 49
[13.] Black, 161-162
[14.] Gould, 215
[15.] Anderson, 201
[16.] Wilson, 94-95
[17.] Sternburg, 59
[18.] Black, 179
[19.] William James, *The Varieties of Religious Experience—A Study in Human Nature,* New York: The Modern Library, 1999, 261

20. Shell, 99-100
21. Long Walk, 52
22. Kenneth A. Dening, B.S., M.ED., Frank S. Deyoe, Jr., B.S., Alfred B. Ellison, B.S., *Ambulation, Physical Rehabilitation for Crutch Walkers,* New York: Funk & Wagnalls Company, 1951, x, hereafter Dening
23. Long Walk, 55
24. Kehret, 103
25. Finger, 102
26. Mee, 100-101
27. Oshinsky, 61
28. Williams, 157-159
29. ibid, 159-160
30. Dille, 47
31. Wilson, 31
32. Bruno, 65
33. John F. Pohl, M.D., *Sister Elizabeth Kenny, The Kenny Concept of Infantile Paralysis and Its Treatment,* Minneapolis, Saint Paul: Bruce Publishing Company, 1943, 17
34. ibid, 19-20
35. ibid, 20-21
36. ibid, 23
37. Rogers, 162
38. Finger, 101
39. Bruno, 72-73
40. Rogers, 47-48
41. ibid, 44-61
42. ibid, 69
43. ibid, 66-67
44. ibid, 90-91
45. ibid, 165
46. ibid, 204
47. ibid, 368-369
48. ibid, 379-381

3. Coming Home

[1.] Dille, 79
[2.] ibid, 85
[3.] ibid, 88
[4.] Wilson, 169-173
[5.] ibid, 179
[6.] Anderson, 209-210
[7.] Shell, 85
[8.] Bruno, 87
[9.] Finger, 162-163
[10.] Anderson, 216
[11.] ibid, 211
[12.] ibid, 237
[13.] Black, 155
[14.] Finger, 258
[15.] ibid, 259
[16.] ibid, 193
[17.] ibid, 226
[18.] Anderson, 188-194
[19.] Finger, 98
[20.] Bruno, 99
[21.] Wilson, 134
[22.] Black, 134
[23.] Sternburg, 92-95
[24.] ibid, 113-130
[25.] ibid, 205
[26.] Beisser, 128
[27.] ibid, 52-67
[28.] Long Walk, 125
[29.] Kriegel, 35
[30.] Long Walk, 227-228
[31.] ibid, 150-172
[32.] ibid, 148
[33.] Kriegel, 41
[34.] Leonard Kriegel, *Falling into life, essays by Leonard*

Kriegel, San Francisco: North Point Press, 1991, 57-59, hereafter Kriegel essays

[35.] Kriegel, 138-139

[36.] Anderson, 116

[37.] Mee, 122

[38.] Anderson, 22

[39.] Black, 154

[40.] ibid, 182-183

[41.] ibid, 157

[42.] Gould, 297-299

[43.] ibid, 300

[44.] ibid, 209

[45.] Shell, 221

[46.] ibid, 219

[47.] ibid, 213

[48.] ibid, 220

[49.] ibid, 130-132

[50.] ibid, 137

[51.] Wilson, 163

[52.] Kehret, 172

[53.] Shell, 34-126

[54.] Anderson, 57

[55.] Black, 137

[56.] Beisser, 144

[57.] ibid, 145-147

[58.] ibid, 148-149

[59.] Mee, 121

[60.] Dille, 162

[61.] Shell, 226

[62.] Black, 247

[63.] Beisser, 187

4. FDR and The March of Dimes

[1.] Nathan Miller, *FDR, An Intimate History*, Lanham, New York, London: Madison Books, 1983, 15-21,

hereafter Miller
2. ibid, 23-27
3. ibid, 31-34
4. ibid, 36
5. ibid, 41-42
6. ibid, 41-51
7. James Tobin, *The Man He Became, How FDR Defied Polio to Win the Presidency,* New York: Simon & Schuster, 13, hereafter Tobin
8. ibid, 13-37
9. ibid, 35
10. Williams, 39
11. Tobin, 38-39
12. ibid, 32
13. ibid, 28
14. ibid, 47-48
15. ibid, 51
16. Gould, 33
17. Tobin, 66-69
18. ibid, 70-76
19. ibid, 80-95
20. ibid, 103-110
21. ibid, 113-119
22. ibid, 133
23. ibid, 134-137
24. ibid, 153-162
25. ibid, 169-172
26. ibid, 174-175
27. ibid, 178
28. ibid, 186-191
29. ibid, 192-195
30. Williams, 123
31. Shell, 182-185
32. Black, 24
33. Oshinsky, 35
34. Tobin, 220-225

35. ibid, 241-249
36. ibid, 250
37. ibid, 251
38. ibid, 255-261
39. ibid, 264-274
40. ibid, 275-288
41. ibid, 297-298
42. ibid, 306-308
43. Richard Carter, *Breakthrough, The Saga of Jonas Salk,* Published simultaneously in the United States and Canada by Trident Press Affiliated Publishers, a Division of Pocket Books, Inc., 1965, 16
44. Jane B. Smith, *Patenting the Sun, Polio and the Salk Vaccine,* New York: William Morrow and Company, Inc., 1990, 65, hereafter Smith
45. ibid, 66-67
46. ibid, 73-75
47. Williams, 123-124
48. Shell, 182-185
49. Williams, 123-124
50. Oshinsky, 64-67
51. ibid, 65
52. Wilson, 139
53. Black, 100-102
54. ibid, 219
55. ibid, 106-108
56. Oshinsky, 83
57. Shell, 113
58. Oshinsky, 88-89
59. ibid, 64-65
60. *The Baltimore Sun,* Wednesday, January 31, 1950
61. *The Baltimore Sun,* December 5, 1952
62. *The Baltimore Sun,* August, 1954, Mary Beth Smith's scrapbook
63. *The Baltimore Sun,* April 8, 1956
64. Anderson, 56

65. ibid, 17
66. ibid, 139
67. ibid, 223
68. ibid, 259
69. Dille, 67-71
70. Anderson, 269

5. The Vaccine

1. Gould, 123
2. Carter, 298
3. Williams, 170-171
4. ibid, 173-174
5. ibid, 105-106
6. ibid, 276-277
7. Carter, 23
8. Roger Vaughan, *Listen to the Music, The Life of Hilary Koprowski,* New York: Springer Science & Business Media, New York: 2000, 46, hereafter Vaughan
9. Oshinsky, 58
10. Carter, 23
11. Oshinsky, 59
12. Smith, 113-114
13. ibid, 113-114
14. ibid, 147
15. Gould, 121
16. Oshinsky, 6
17. Williams, 111
18. Oshinsky, 128
19. Williams, 187
20. *Philadelphia Inquirer,* April 13, 2013
21. Vaughan, 4
22. ibid, 59-66
23. ibid, 100
24. ibid, 27-33
25. Williams, 220-225

26. Vaughan, 36-40
27. ibid, 44-45
28. ibid, 5-13
29. ibid, 15
30. ibid, 16
31. ibid, 49
32. ibid, 50
33. ibid, 73-90
34. ibid, 93
35. ibid, 147-148
36. ibid, 195
37. ibid, 197
38. ibid, 247-262
39. ibid, 227-228
40. , ibid, 225
41. ibid, 229-230
42. Carter, 137
43. ibid, 66
44. Oshinsky, 169
45. ibid, 95
46. Carter, 28-33
47. ibid, 34-35
48. Smith, 102-106
49. Oshinsky, 102-110
50. Williams, 192-193
51. Oshinsky, 102-107
52. Smith, 98-99
53. Carter, 58-59
54. Smith, 108-110
55. Carter, 64
56. ibid, 73
57. Smith, 120-121
58. Gould, 322-323
59. Carter, 60
60. Oshinsky, 123-124
61. Carter, 93

62. ibid, 107-109
63. ibid, 113-121
64. ibid, 113-121
65. ibid, 97
66. Oshinsky, 154-158
67. Smith, 137-141
68. Oshinsky, 161
69. Smith, 176
70. ibid, 186
71. Carter, 156-159
72. ibid, 162-163
73. Smith, 255
74. ibid, 144-145
75. Carter, 209-210
76. ibid, 217-219
77. ibid, 228-229
78. Smith, 225-229
79. Black, 219
80. Carter, 229-230
81. ibid, 238-240
82. Smith, 225-235
83. ibid, 265-273
84. ibid, 236-237
85. ibid, 256-260
86. Oshinsky, 197
87. Smith, 273
88. ibid, 274-287
89. ibid, 290
90. Carter, 242
91. Smith, 299-301
92. Carter, 244-266
93. Smith, 308-309
94. Carter, 267
95. ibid, 267
96. Smith, 322
97. Oshinsky, 201

98. Smith, 302-305
99. Carter, 285-291
100. Smith, 341-343
101. Oshinsky, 215-216
102. Smith, 248-251
103. Carter, 282
104. Williams, 211
105. Oshinsky, 235
106. Carter, 309-317
107. Smith, 360-362
108. Carter, 319-324
109. ibid, 327
110. ibid, 327-330
111. ibid, 331-332
112. Smith, 367-369
113. Carter, 400-401
114. ibid, 501-502
115. Gould, 294-295
116. Smith, 373
117. Carter, 351
118. Roger Rapoport, *The Super-Doctors,* Chicago: Playboy Press, 1975, 249-250, hereafter Superdoctors
119. Smith, 375-377
120. Williams, 216-219
121. Oshinsky, 138
122. Williams, 231
123. Vaughan, 53
124. Oshinsky, 138-139
125. Williams, 231-235
126. Oshinsky, 244
127. ibid, 143-246
128. Williams, 236-238
129. Oshinsky, 243-251
130. ibid, 252-283
131. ibid, 256-268
132. Carter, 380

133. ibid, 347
134. Smith, 385-386
135. Superdoctors, 254-257
136. Carter, 392-393
137. Oshinsky, 278-279
138. Williams, 282
139. Rogers, 402
140. Oshinsky, 271-273
141. Gould, 187
142. Oshinsky, 290-291
143. Williams, 263
144. ibid, 290-291

6. Post-Polio Syndrome (PPS)

1. Shell, 34
2. Anderson, 227-228
3. Gould, 206
4. ibid, 209-213
5. Oshinsky, 284-285
6. ibid, 232-233
7. Bruno, 30-33
8. ibid, 17
9. ibid, 133-170
10. ibid, xx-4
11. Williams, 34
12. Shell, 176
13. Wilson, 236-241
14. Anderson, 245-250
15. ibid, 132-133
16. ibid, 119-120
17. ibid, 149-150
18. ibid, 143
19. Wilson, 234
20. Bruno, 299
21. Anderson, 26-27

22. ibid, 22
23. ibid, 208
24. ibid, 75-76
25. ibid, 43
26. ibid, 273
27. ibid, 140-162
28. Wilson, 234
29. Kriegel essays, 109
30. ibid, 116-118
31. ibid, 110
32. Dille, 156-161
33. Finger, 122
34. ibid, 265

7. Dad

1. Beisser, 12
2. Abraham H. Maslow, *Motivation and Personality*, New York, Evanston, and London: Harper & Row, Publishers, 1970, 137
3. ibid, 157
4. ibid, 159
5. ibid, 160
6. ibid, 168
7. ibid, 169
8. ibid, 171

Bibliography

Connie Anderson, editor, *How Ordinary People Overcame Extraordinary Challenges,* Minneapolis, MN: CAB Press, 2013

The Baltimore Sun, Wednesday, January 31, 1950

The Baltimore Sun, December 5, 1952

The Baltimore Sun, August, 1954, Mary Beth Smith's scrapbook

The Baltimore Sun, April 8, 1956

Arnold Beisser, *Flying Without Wings, Personal Reflections on Loss, Disability, and Healing,* New York, Toronto, London, Sydney, Auckland: 1990

Kathryn Black, *In the Shadow of Polio, A Personal and Social History,* Reading, Massachusetts: Addison-Wesley Publishing Company, 1996

Richard L. Bruno, H.D., PhD, *The Polio Paradox, Uncovering the Hidden History of Polio to Understand and Treat "Post-Polio Syndrome" and Chronic Fatigue,* New York: Warner Books, Inc. 2002

Richard Carter, *Breakthrough, The Saga of Jonas Salk,* Published simultaneously in the United States and

Canada by Trident Press Affiliated Publishers, a Division of Pocket Books, Inc., 1965

Kenneth A. Dening, B.S., M.ED., Frank S. Deyoe, Jr., B.S., Alfred B. Ellison, B.S., *Ambulation, Physical Rehabilitation for Crutch Walkers,* New York: Funk & Wagnalls Company, 1951

Jeane L. Curey Dille, *Polio: A Dose of the Refiner's Fire, Surviving Polio,* Bloomington, Indiana: authorHOUSE, 2005

Anne Finger, *Elegy For A Disease, a Personal and Cultural History of Polio,* New York: St.Martin's Press, 2006

Tony Gould, *A Summer Plague, Polio and its Survivors,* New Haven & London: Yale University Press, 1995

William James, *The Varieties of Religious Experience—A Study in Human Nature,* New York: The Modern Library, 1999

Peg Kehret, *Small Steps: The Year I Got Polio,* Morton Grove, Illinois: Albert Whitman & Company, 1996

Leonard Kriegel, *Falling into life, essays by Leonard Kriegel,* San Francisco: North Point Press, 1991

Leonard Kriegel, *Flying Solo, Reimagining Manhood, Courage, and Loss,* Boston: Beacon Press, 1998

Leonard Kriegel, *The Long Walk Home,* New York: Appleton-century Affiliate of Meredith Press Van Rees Press, 1964

Abraham H. Maslow, *Motivation and Personality,* New York, Evanston, and London: Harper & Row, Publishers, 1970

Charles L. Mee, *A Nearly Normal Life, a memoir,* Boston, Little, Brown and Company, 1999

Nathan Miller, *FDR, An Intimate History,* Lanham, New York, London: Madison Books, 1983

David M. Oshinsky, *Polio, An American Story,* New York: Oxford University Press: 2005

Philadelphia Inquirer, April 13, 2013

John F. Pohl,, M.D., *Sister Elizabeth Kenny, The Kenny Concept of Infantile Paralysis and Its Treatment,* Minneapolis, Saint Paul: Bruce Publishing Company, 1943

Roger Rapoport, *The Super-Doctors,* Chicago: Playboy Press, 1975

Guenter B. Risse, Revolt Against Quarantine: Community Responses to the 1916 Polio Epidemic, Oyster Bay, New York – Transactions & Studies of the College of Physicians of Philadelphia, Ser. 5, Vol. 114, No. 1 (1992); 23-50 copyright 1992 by the College of Physicians of Philadelphia

Naomi Rogers, *Polio Wars, Sister Elizabeth Kenny and the Golden Age of American Medicine,* New York: Oxford University Press, 2014

Marc Shell, *Polio and its Aftermath, The Paralysis of Culture,* Cambridge, Mass: President and Fellows of Harvard College, 2005

Jane B. Smith, *Patenting the Sun, Polio and the Salk Vaccine,* New York: William Morrow and Company, Inc., 1990

Mary Beth Smith, *Healing Manic Depression and Depression, What Works, Based on What Helped Me,* amazon.com, 2013

Mary Beth Smith, *The Joy of Life, A Biography of Theodore Roosevelt,* amazon.com, 2013

Louis and Dorothy Sternburg with Monica Dickens, *View from the Seesaw,* New York: Dodd, Mead & Company, 1986

James Tobin, *The Man He Became, How FDR Defied Polio to Win the Presidency,* New York: Simon & Schuster

Roger Vaughan, *Listen to the Music, The Life of Hilary Koprowski,* New York: Springer Science & Business Media, New York: 2000

Gareth Williams, *Paralysed with Fear, The Story of Polio,* Palgrave: MacMillan, 2013

Daniel J. Wilson, *Living with Polio, The Epidemic and Its Survivors,* Chicago: The University of Chicago Press, 2005

About the Author

MARY BETH SMITH was born and raised near Towson, Maryland. She graduated from Notre Dame of Maryland University. She worked as a programmer/analyst for 20 years until she went on disability in 1995. Her father, H. Edwin Jones, was a survivor of the polio epidemic of 1944 and held positions in the National Foundation for Infantile Paralysis (NFIP) for over ten years. He became chairman of the Baltimore Chapter of the NFIP in 1956. He retired as head of the last vegetable cannery in Baltimore at age 62 after he became weak with post-polio syndrome. He was an inspiration to all Baltimore polio survivors.

Made in the USA
Middletown, DE
07 February 2020